A GUIDE TO FIELD IDENTIFICATION

AMPHIBIANS
OF NORTH AMERICA

by

HOBART M. SMITH

Department of Environmental, Population,
and Organismic Biology
University of Colorado, Boulder

Illustrated by
SY BARLOWE

 GOLDEN PRESS • NEW YORK

WESTERN PUBLISHING COMPANY, INC.
RACINE, WISCONSIN

PREFACE

This book has been long in the making since first conceived in the mid sixties, has undergone major conceptual shifts since initiated, and has seen knowledge of the North American amphibian fauna burgeon. For those intrigued by a dynamic, changing field, the study of amphibians has much to offer. Although a large body of established facts has been amassed, much remains to be learned about these in many ways still mysterious animals. It is hoped that readers will be encouraged to make their own contributions to the exploration of amphibian natural history, one of the few remaining frontiers of vertebrate zoology in North America.

Without the generous aid of colleagues and the basic work of predecessors, even so preliminary a survey as this would not have been possible. To Dr. Roger Conant and Dr. Robert Stebbins a special debt is owed for their monumental role in summarizing over the past half century the advancing state of our knowledge of the taxonomy, distribution, and variation of North American amphibians. The counsel and generous sharing of color slides and other source material for artwork from many other colleagues have been vital; we acknowledge with gratitude the aid especially of Dr. Kraig Adler, Dr. Ronald Altig, Dr. Albert Blair, Mrs. Beatrice Boone, Dr. Arden Brame, Dr. Ronald Brandon, Dr. Edmund Brodie, Dr. Lauren Brown, Mr. Robert Brown, Dr. William Brownlee, Mr. David Dennis, Dr. James Dixon, Dr. Kenneth Dodd, Dr. David Easterla, Dr. W. Ronald Heyer, Dr. Richard Highton, Mr. Richard Holland, Dr. Floyd Potter, Dr. Samuel Sweet, Dr. Robert Thomas, and Dr. David Wake.

It has been my good fortune to benefit from the skillful and patient guidance, dedication to excellence, and creativity of Barbara Williams, this book's primary editor. Important contributions were also made by Roger Menges, Vera Webster, and George Fichter. The skill and devotion to accuracy of Sy Barlowe and his talented wife, Dorothea, have been outstanding. And to Rozella Smith there is a special debt of infinite diversity.

H.M.S.

TABLE OF CONTENTS

AMPHIBIANS—class Amphibia

COLOR KEY FOR RANGE MAPS

The range of each species north of Mexico is shown by a color area (or areas) on the maps. When there are subspecies, different colors are used within the area to indicate which portion of the total range each subspecies inhabits. Numbers in the following key refer to the numbers used in the text to designate each subspecies.

  Subspecies (1).   ☐ Subspecies (3).   ◻ Subspecies (6).

■ Subspecies (2).   ■ Subspecies (4).   ◨ Subspecies (7).

■ Subspecies (5).

INTRODUCING AMPHIBIANS

This book is a guide to the identification of frogs, toads, and salamanders native to North America north of Mexico. A total of 15 families, 32 genera, 178 species and 270 subspecies are treated. Among them are four foreign species introduced since the settlement of North America by Europeans.

Frogs, toads, and salamanders—known collectively as *amphibians*—with few exceptions spend their lives partly in water, partly on land. But even on land they require ample moisture. For that reason they tend to cluster in damper areas, so that population density over the continent varies radically. Where the climate is favorably wet, more individuals live, also more kinds of individuals. Thus both population density and species variety are greatest in the southern United States and other regions of heavy rainfall. Georgia's Okefenokee Swamp, for example, teems with frogs, toads, and salamanders numbering in the millions per square mile. Georgia alone boasts 64 different amphibian species, Alabama 61, Texas 60, Florida 48. In contrast, cool, dry high-latitude and high-altitude areas support few species and only sparse populations—a few thousand individuals per square mile at most. Thus the states of the semi-arid midcontinent are home to relatively few amphibians; Colorado has 16 species, Utah 12, North Dakota only 11. In all the vast expanse of Canada there are only 39, and in Alaska only six.

Regional differences in population density and number of species are even more pronounced among salamanders than among frogs and toads. The presence of salamander species in a given region is correlated not only with high humidity and tolerable temperature but also with historically non-glaciated mountain streams. Because most mountainous locales of Colorado and Wyoming were ice-covered until the end of the last glacial epoch about 10,000 years ago, today those highlands are inhabited by only one salamander species, the Tiger. In fact, vast areas of the midwestern and southwestern United States are host to that species alone. But in the Appalachian area there are more salamander species than anywhere else in North America; the next greatest profusion occurs in the Sierra Nevada area.

All amphibians are predatory carnivores as adults, feeding largely on small worms and on arthropods—insects, spiders, millipedes, and the like. The population densities of these invertebrate creatures, particularly in warm humid regions, defies calculation. Since every amphibian dines on many invertebrates every day, countless billions fall victim to amphibian appetite. The world benefits both directly and indirectly from this relentless predation. But while such voracious insect control may alone be reason enough to protect amphibians, there is also the simple fact of humankind's responsibility for its biotic

5

legacy. To give frogs, toads, and salamanders their needed protection, we must know them, understand them. This guide is intended to promote such comprehension through observation in the field, and to help bring about a proprietary interest in amphibian welfare on the part of amateurs as well as professionals. Besides, field study of frogs, toads, and salamanders is matchless fun.

Where Amphibians Live

Amphibians are fascinating creatures. Their curious habits and unique physical characteristics have evolved over millions of years as survival adaptations in a ruthlessly competitive world where reptiles and mammals dominate the land, fishes the water, and birds the air. A study in resourcefulness, amphibians survive in transitional marginal areas, called ecotones, that lie between the domains of terrestrial animals and the habitat of aquatic creatures. There is no major habitat amphibians can call their own.

They breed where they live, rarely wandering more than short distances. The kinds that favor permanent bodies of water, for example, do not stray far from the lakes or streams of their birth. No great travelers either are the numerous amphibian groups that shun permanent freshwater locales, favoring temporary rain pools, swampy morasses, rills, drainage waters, seepages, irrigation flows. Even the traces of moisture encountered in rock crevices may be enough to support some forms of amphibian life. A few amphibian species, able to climb bushes and trees, spend considerable periods aloft. Almost all frogs and toads—and certain salamanders as well—can bury themselves in soil. Some are capable of burrowing to depths of several feet where they may live in a state of suspended animation, if necessary, for several years. Species unable to burrow may take up residence in the digs of other animals—or settle down in cracks, crevices, or holes worn in earth or rock by water and weather.

When and Where to Look

Except at mating time, when male frogs and toads utter their calls singly or in chorus, amphibians are rarely seen or heard. Indeed, the sudden appearance in wet weather of frogs in great numbers, seemingly out of nowhere, led ancient peoples to believe the creatures fell from the sky with the rains. Today we know they are always with us but during most of the year keep themselves concealed, especially by day, to escape predation and dehydration. Yet even though amphibians stay well hidden most of the time, individuals of many species can be uncovered by appropriate search regardless of season. The best place to look is in or near water, swampy lands, moist spots. Amphibians commonly hide under natural debris such as fallen leaves, among mossy or moist rocks, in rotting logs. Holes, hollows, crevices of any kind, and tunnel openings should be patiently investigated. Bear in mind that nearly all species are nocturnal, presenting the problem of how to light the hunt. Also, members of some species are found only rarely and more by accident than design—the salamanders that inhabit artesian waters, for instance.

On almost any warm night, frogs and toads can be seen along paved roads, especially during or after rains. In the Rocky Mountain region, Tiger Salamanders as well as frogs and toads appear on roads after rains even in daytime. The salamanders are emerging, after transformation, from ponds and lakes where they spent their larval life. Sometimes amphiumas are seen wriggling across roads during heavy rains in the southeastern United States.

But most species of frogs and toads—together termed *anurans*—convene at permanent or temporary pools to breed, often by the hundreds of thousands. Over most of the continent the largest assemblages take place in spring, generally during or after substantial rainfall. But in the arid or semi-arid regions of the western United States and Canada, the gatherings occur in summer or autumn—whenever the first heavy rains arrive. At such times the males, according to species, call singly or in chorus, singing their hearts out to attract females from near and far. So distinctive are the calls of frogs and toads that, as with birds, the sounds identify the calling species. This is helpful to anuran enthusiasts but even more so to the anurans themselves. The call affords a female instant recognition of males of her own species, thus maintaining species integrity and preventing interbreeding that would result in wasted reproductive effort and breakdown of genetically established adaptations.

The best time to observe and collect anurans, then, is at night during or after spring rains—summer or autumn rain in some parts of the continent. And the best place is near a permanent or temporary body of water. It is an unforgettable experience to wade by lantern light amid a dense chorus of frogs or toads, attending one of nature's greatest symphonies. In frenzied chorus, breeding anurans are so preoccupied that they are virtually oblivious to movements or light around them. On dark nights they can easily be seized and picked up. But on moonlit nights collecting becomes difficult. Apparently by moonlight the animals can see beyond a lamp that otherwise would be blinding. Remember also that small choruses are more readily disturbed and dispersed than large ones.

Finding Salamanders

Salamanders as a group are not as easily found as anurans, mainly because salamanders do not assemble to breeding choruses. Some kinds do congregate to breed, but most reproduce in scattered pairs.

Except for the Tiger, they seldom wander far enough from the breeding site to be encountered on roadsides clearings, or other semi-open places where frogs and toads occasionally are encountered. In the North American East and Far West, salamanders are seen mostly in small streams, usually under stones, pieces of wood, broken tree limbs, or other similar debris; also they may be found in damp places under litter on land near pools or seepages. They prefer forested regions, often hiding in or under rotting logs. Because of their wanderlust, Tiger Salamanders may trap themselves in pits or wells from which they cannot escape, or may loiter in damp cellars.

The truly aquatic salamanders are most easily collected by seining in streams, lakes, or ponds. Sometimes mudpuppies (*Necturus*) and Hellbenders (*Cryptobranchus*) are taken on hook and line, but the risk of injuring them is too great to use the method for capturing specimens for live study.

You will not find salamanders or other amphibians where there are fish, except in shallow, weedy waters that offer places in which the defenseless, developing young may hide from swimming predators. Knowing this narrows greatly the choice of waters eligible for search.

Lights for Collecting

Local conditions, and to a lesser extent personal choice, determine the kind of light used in nocturnal collection of anurans. When among large choruses or proceeding along roads or other open areas, the wide illumination provided by a gasoline lantern serves best; the single-mantle type is quite adequate and less tiring to carry. Such a lantern gives free range to peripheral vision. When searching over a broad area, hold the lantern close to the chest so that the hood deflects the light from your eyes and also conceals your body by shading it. On moonlit nights, or when amphibians are not abundant, a headlamp or floodlight with a concentrated beam is the most useful. The beam can be directed at specific targets with little disturbance to surrounding areas and if necessary be quickly extinguished. Also, very little of your body is revealed to alarm the animals.

The eyes of larger species of anurans glow in a light beam like reddish reflectors and can be perceived at distances of 50 feet of more. Eyes of smaller species do not shine distinctly, or the shine is easily confused with the myriad of similar smaller reflections evoked by a strong light. Spider eyes, for example, often cast an astonishingly bright glow. Small frogs can be detected only by their body form, exasperatingly difficult to make out in the dark. An elusive singing frog is most easily located by triangulation, for which two searchers are needed. Walking a few feet apart, each can direct his beam toward the apparent source of the sound. The frog will be found where the beams cross.

Other Collecting Gear

Unbleached muslin bags of various sizes, double-sewed with round corners to eliminate loose, entangling threads, make excellent containers. They should be about half again as deep as wide and be fitted with a tie string about two inches from the top. Muslin bags do not break even when wet and so can safely hold moist litter, thus reducing dehydration of captured amphibians. The bags can be carried looped under the belt, leaving both hands free. Aquatic stages of amphibians, whether larvae or adults, must be carried in leakproof containers— plastic preferred, glass only if there is no other choice—with some of the water in which they were living.

Knee or hip boots or sometimes even waders are desirable, particularly in cold weather, if it is necessary to negotiate streams, lakes, or ponds. Leather boots and jeans are comfortable for wading in warm weather. Gloves protect against irritating secretions.

For collecting aquatic larvae or adults, a seine is needed. About 10 by 12 feet and 3 feet deep is a good size. Using a seine requires two people. The seine can be tied between poles that become the handles, or each person can place one foot in the loop in the lower string of the seine while holding the upper string in his hand. Seining is done by day. Boards, logs, stones, or other bottom debris under which amphibians might hide are turned. If there is a current, the net is spread downstream so that the animals wash into the net when the objects are lifted. A potato hook is useful for turning debris either in water or on land. It reduces the amount of stooping and also minimizes the possibility of contact with poisonous plants or animals.

Ethics for the Enthusiast

A cardinal rule: always replace disturbed surface litter so that it can continue to serve as sanctuary. Try to leave the search area as close to its original, undisturbed condition as you can manage. Collect no more than you need, and when finished examining and observing the animals, return them to as near the site of capture as possible. In home territory they have a better chance for survival; besides, by returning them you help maintain the balance in locally adaptive gene pools. Remember to ask permission before collecting on private property. Refusals are rare, but permission in advance can prevent embarrassing confrontatons or even fines for trespassing. Acquaint yourself with state regulations, if any, governing collections of amphibians. Above all, consult your state fish and wildlife service to learn which species in the locality are on the endangered list. For information on the care of captive specimens, see p. 147.

TOPOGRAPHY

Frogs and Toads

Anurans (frogs and toads) are essentially of one basic body form. All lack a tail, except for a vestige in the Tailed Toad (*Ascaphus truei*). All have four legs. The hind legs, each with five digits, are longer and stronger than the forelegs, each with four digits. Just behind the middle of the back, there is a pronounced hump where the vertebral column joins the pelvic girdle at the sacrum. All anurans possess well-developed lidded eyes and paired though diminutive nostrils.

Different families of anurans are distinguished by characteristic sets of structures, as illustrated on pages 11 and 12. Most species of true frogs (family Ranidae) have two dorsolateral "folds" (really ridges) that vary in length according to species. In the Bullfrog (*Rana catesbyiana*), the fold curls over the tympanum (eardrum) and ends just above the forelegs. Anuran feet are long, the toes extensively webbed. A few smooth ridges or warts may occur on the moist skin. Males differ from females in having a thickened, sometimes darkened inner surface on the "thumb" and, in some species, a larger tympanum.

True toads (family Bufonidae) have a dry skin. An exception is the Colorado River Toad (*Bufo alvarius*), whose skin is moist to the touch. All toads show a distinct swelling, a parotoid gland, on each side of the neck. The parotoids and other wartlike glands in the skin produce a foul-tasting poison that discourages predators, may even be lethal to them if toads are eaten. Most true toads have cranial crests (see illustration). Distinctive features of males include the horny inner surface of the thumb (sometimes also the second digit) and a dark throat associated with one or two vocal sacs. The sac, which inflates only when the toad is calling, differs in shape with the species. True toads also have two hard, often black tubercles at the base of each forefoot and hind foot—the metacarpal and metatarsal tubercles, respectively. In identification, it is important to distinguish the inner and outer metatarsal tubercles.

A third set of distinctive characters defines the spadefoot toads (*Scaphiopus* and *Spea*). They have moist skin, two black metatarsal tubercles, and vertical pupils (horizontal or round in all other anurans). In males, the thumb and often the second toe are horny.

Still another set of characters distinguishes the Bell Toad (*Ascaphus truei*): moist skin, lack of a visible tympanum, and, most important, a tail-like projection larger in males than in females. Males are recognizable also by horny growth on thumb and forefoot.

Treefrogs (family Hylidae) all have an intercalary cartilage between the last and next-to-last phalanges (bones) of each toe. This unique identifying feature is seen best by looking at any digit from the side rather than from above or below. In this family many species have an

BODY FORMS OF FROGS AND TOADS

TOP OF HEAD
nostril
eye
cranial crest
parotoid gland
tympanum
warts

nostril
eye mask
tympanum
ridges
hump

4 toes on forefeet
moist skin

TRUE FROG

5 toes on hind feet
webbing

dry skin
glands on leg
typanum
parotoid gland
warts

TRUE TOAD

inner tubercle
outer tubercle
inner tubercle
FOREFOOT

outer tubercle

HIND FOOT

vertical pupil

metatarsal tubercles

SPADEFOOT TOAD

light band

♀

"tail"

horny growths
moist skin

♂

"tail"

BELL TOAD

moist skin
tympanum

TREEFROG

chest fold
pleated throat skin

large discs

phalanges
adhesive disc
intercalary cartilage

moist skin
no webs
disc

NARROW-TOED TOAD
slight webbing

tiny head
broad waist
short legs

skin fold
smooth skin
metatarsal tubercles

NARROW-MOUTHED TOAD

expanded pad at the tip of each digit but in some the pad is minute or absent, as in the Cricket Frog (*Acris*) and chorus frogs (*Pseudacris*). In all species the skin is moist, the tympanum visible, and the waist slender. Males of some species have thickened thumbs or pleated throat skin (over the inflatable vocal sac), or both.

Narrow-toed toads (family Leptodactylidae) bear a distinctive fold of skin around the ventral edge of the entire abdomen, forming a disclike surface. The skin is moist, the digits completely web-free.

The most oddly shaped anurans are the tiny-headed, broad-waisted, short-legged sheep toads (*Hypopachus*), narrow-mouthed toads (*Gastrophryne*), and the Cone-nosed Toad (*Rhinophrynus dorsalis*). All have smooth skin and two conspicuous heel (metatarsal) tubercles. The Cone-nosed Toad lacks a visible tympanum; the others have a fold of skin across the rear of the head.

Salamanders

All salamanders except newts are distinguished by costal grooves, and all have eyelids. Most have five digits on the hind feet. Exceptions are the slender salamanders (*Batrachoseps*), the Dwarf Salamander (*Manculus quadridigitatus*), and the Four-toed Salamander (*Hemidactylium scutatum*), all with four hind digits. Like anurans, salamanders make do with only four toes on the front feet. Transformed adults do not have external gills. A few species may breed as larvae. Such individuals are said to be *neotenic*.

Adult salamanders in North America occur in five body forms. Except for a few species in the first or "standard" group, in which transformation takes place in the egg, all salamanders go through a gilled larval stage.

The standard form of salamander has a more or less lizardlike body with four legs longer than the body is wide. The body and tail vary from elongate and slender with the legs a sixth of the head-plus-body length—as in the California Slender Salamander (*Batrachoseps*

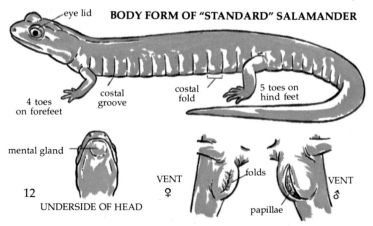

BODY FORM OF "STANDARD" SALAMANDER

eye lid

costal groove

costal fold

5 toes on hind feet

4 toes on forefeet

mental gland

VENT ♀

folds

VENT ♂

papillae

UNDERSIDE OF HEAD

12

attenuatus)—to short and fat with the legs a third of the head-plus-body length—as in the Mole Salamander (*Ambystoma talpoideum*).

The external features of an idealized standard salamander are illustrated below left. Only males in the family Plethodontidae have a mental gland. But the rest of the structures of the standard salamander are found in most salamanders of the other four body forms. In all forms the vent is longitudinal, but costal grooves and folds are lacking in a few species. Although differences between male and female vary with the species, breeding males commonly can be distinguished by minute projections (papillae) that line the vent and by the surrounding glandular swelling. Females show little or no swelling and no papillae, but the vent lining may be ridged.

Mudpuppies (*Necturus*) have a second kind of body form, much like the standard but with gills retained throughout life, only four digits on the hind feet, and no movable eyelids. These creatures are stout-bodied and rather sizable, reportedly attaining lengths of up to 17 inches (43.2 mm).

The Hellbender (*Cryptobranchus alleganiensis*) manifests a third body form, also much like the standard but with the skin bunching in loose folds at the sides and rear edges of the limbs. Hellbenders lack eyelids, and are one of the few species bare of costal grooves or folds. The head is broad and flat, with a gill slit (but no gills) on one or both sides of the neck. The legs are short and stout.

Amphiumas (genus *Amphiuma*), representing the fourth body form, have four diminutive limbs less than half as long as the body is wide, one gill slit on each side (but no gills), no eyelids, and no more than three digits on each limb. The body is cylindrical, elongated, and eel-like. Amphiumas can become extremely large; specimens nearly 46 inches long (116.2 cm) are known.

Sirens (*Siren*), the fifth body form, superficially resemble amphiumas, being relatively long and cylindrical. But the Siren has neither eyelids nor hind limbs. Its external gills lie close to the forelegs, which terminate in the usual four digits.

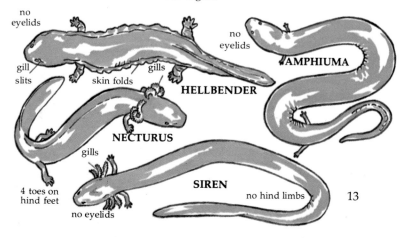

no eyelids

no eyelids

AMPHIUMA

gill slits

gills

skin folds

HELLBENDER

NECTURUS

gills

4 toes on hind feet

SIREN

no hind limbs

no eyelids

13

AMPHIBIAN NAMES

Amphibian common names are not yet fully standardized. They may vary from region to region or be applied arbitrarily by authorities according to individual preference. In this book each species is designated by both a common and a scientific name (in parentheses). If well established, common names serve better for identification because they are handy and mean more to more people. In bird identification, for example, common names are preferred by professionals as well as amateurs. But for positive identification of amphibians, whose common names are not always well established, professionals rely on scientific names—and amateurs should do likewise. Besides, the scientific nomenclature helps to pinpoint relationships among amphibians at their various hierarchal levels.

Species and Subspecies

A *species* is a genetically distinctive population of individuals isolated reproductively from all other populations of individuals. A *subspecies* is a population segment of a species and occupies a particular portion of the range of that species. More than one subspecies of a given species never occurs in a single locality (unless they are end populations of a species with a circular range—a rare condition). Species and subspecies are natural entities. All other divisions in the hierarchy of classification are conceptual, "man made" groupings that indicate degrees of similarity of species populations.

Scientific names for species consist of two words—first the generic name (genus) and then the specific name (species). Thus *Rana pipiens* is the scientific name of the species known by the common name of Northern Leopard Frog, meaning that it is of the genus *Rana* and has been specifically designated *pipiens*. Note that the generic name begins with a capital letter, the specific name does not, and both names are italicized.

Subspecies bear a three-word scientific name, the subspecies name being tacked on to the two words of the species name. For example, one subspecies of *Rana clamitans* (the Green Frog) has been dubbed *melanota,* so its complete scientific name is *Rana clamitans melanota.*

Higher Category Names

Above the level of species, scientific names consist of a single word. Both the Leopard Frog and the Green Frog belong to the genus *Rana* in the family Ranidae (names above the genus level are not italicized). Family names are based on the name of a member genus. Some families are comprised of only one genus; others contain many.

The basic classification categories, in descending order, are: kingdom, phylum, class, order, family, genus, and species. Each division in this rigidly hierarchical system usually contains subdivisions.

All animals in this book belong to the class Amphibia, represented in North America by the order Salientia (or Anura), consisting of frogs and toads, collectively referred to as anurans, or tail-less amphibians—and by the order Caudata, consisting of salamanders.

Kinds of Variation

Varied physical forms occur within groups at every classification level. This variability of body characters is termed *diversity*. Kinds of variation include:

Clinal variation. This is common in species that inhabit a wide climatic range, either vertical as on mountain slopes or horizontal as on extensive plains. For example, legs of the Wood Frog are shorter in Canada and longer toward the southern U.S., indicating horizontal clinal variation.

Intergradation. This variation occurs in offspring where the respective ranges of subspecies adjoin. Specifically, intergradation describes a blending of the characters of two (or more) subspecies not completely separated geographically—on islands, for example. In such cases the animals interbreed freely but maintain separate group identities because of their genetic adaptations to a particular environment.

Hybridization. This term refers to production of *hybrids*—that is, offspring of parents from differing groups. Generally the term is applied only to offspring of parents of different species. Under some conditions, hybridization can occur between individuals of different genera and even different families. Still, hybrids are rare in nature and produced only under unusual circumstances. Hybrids exhibit combinations of distinctive features of the two parent species.

Age variations. These, as mentioned earlier, can make identification difficult. After transformation from the larval stage, the colors, markings, and conformations of the mature adult take time to develop. Thus the identifying features of the species may not be visible in younger adults.

Sex variations. In a majority of species, mature males and females tend to look alike; in some species they show differences. This book gives the differences if they are pertinent to identification. Of course, the voiceless anuran female does not have the vocal sacs of her suitors—but in most species she tends to be larger than they are.

Other notable variations are *albinism*, meaning lack of *melanin* (dark pigment normally present in skin); *melanism*, meaning excess of melanin; and *partial albinism* or *partial melanism*, lying between the species norm and either extreme. *Morphs*, which occur in some species, are sharply distinctive color- or pattern-types with few or no intermediate characters.

HOW TO USE THIS BOOK

This guide focuses on the identification of adult amphibians. Concise information and precise illustrations are presented, enabling you to determine the species of all frogs, toads, and salamanders you may encounter in the field. The material is organized in a manner that speeds and simplifies the identifying process; text, pictures, and maps pertaining to a given species run side by side. To take full advantage of this streamlined scheme, it is suggested that you proceed as follows:

1. Scan the illustrations for one that matches the specimen—an obvious first step that may result in immediate identification.

2. If no illustration yields positive identification, re-scan to find an illustrated group (family, genus, species) with which the specimen shares one or more physical characteristics (color, markings, anatomical features, etc.).

3. Inspect the range maps for that group. The maps tell you which species occur where you found your specimen. (Color key on p. 4.)

4. Consult the species descriptions next to the maps. This narrows your choices until, by elimination, you arrive at the most likely identification—or more than one likely identification.

5. Verify the identification, or select among possible identifications, by using the keys.

Identifying by Key

Keys are shortcuts to positive identification. They work by utilizing the presence or absence of "key" characteristics to eliminate one candidate species after another until only the valid choice remains. Although not infallible, keys rank among the important tools of the professional. When easy to use, like the condensed keys in this book, they can be valuable to the amateur as well. Begin by consulting the anuran key (p. 22) or the salamander key (p. 72) to determine the specimen's family. Those keys will lead you either to the pages where an identification can be made or to a second key. The second key may provide the identification or, in a few cases, direct you to a third and final key.

Suppose, for example, your specimen's toes are unwebbed, indicating it is one of the narrow-toed toads (family Leptodactylidae). The key to the narrow-toed toads (p. 28) starts as follows:

1. Whitish streak along upper lip ....
.... **White-lipped,** p. 30
No such streak ....*see* 2
2. Skin fold on each side of back ......
.... **Barking,** p. 30
No skin fold on back ....*see* 3

Select the most fitting statement in the first numbered couplet; this leads you to either the common name of your specimen or a boldface number that directs you to the next couplet to be consulted. Continue in that fashion until you arrive at a common name.

Illustrations accompany the keys. Color in those illustrations symbolizes, rather than portrays, the actual hues and tints of the animals.

After determining the species, you may narrow the identification further by checking the brief distinguishing characters of the subspecies described in the text. For some species, no subspecies are currently recognized; others have two or more—as many as seven for the Tiger Salamander, five for the Gopher Frog. The range maps help you identify subspecies, since different subspecies of the same species almost never occupy the same locality (see p. 14). Where intergrades occur (see p. 15), they are best labeled only to the species names; if named to subspecies, the name should reflect the two or more subspecies involved—for example, *Bufo debilis debilis x insidior.*

Policies of the Book

1. The sequence followed in presenting families and genera reflects their evolutionary development, going from least advanced to most advanced. Arrangement of species within those groups, however, is governed by considerations of clarity and space limitations.

2. To avoid complexity, only the most salient characters of subspecies are noted. Many herpetologists rank subspecies with species and give each a common name. But in this book, subspecies are treated as in most branches of vertebrate zoology; that is, they are regarded as secondary in rank to species—which indeed is the case—and so are not given common names. If the species is known, usually the subspecies can be identified by its locality. Therefore, the various common names ascribed to subspecies by various experts are superfluous and tend to confuse.

3. The entire range of each species north of Mexico is given by the range maps. Ranges of subspecies are indicated as portions of the total range of the species, shown by the use of different colors. A key to the colors used on the maps is given on p. 4.

4. Illustrations depict adults unless otherwise noted. Where helpful, subspecies are illustrated. Supplementary illustrations show significant variations or details and, in a few instances, sexual differences. The male is designated by the symbol ♂, the female by ♀.

5. Dimensions are given in both inches and millimeters, with fractional inches rounded off to the millimeter equivalents. Sizes listed are the reported maximums for the species.

6. Counts given in the text for costal grooves and folds apply to those on one side of a salamander only.

AMPHIBIANS—class Amphibia

Amphibians of North America north of Mexico belong to two major groups: the frogs and toads (order Salientia) and the salamanders (order Caudata). A third group, the caecilians (order Gymnophiona), lives only in the tropics. Unlike reptiles, amphibians have clawless toes and thin moist skin. Since they readily lose water through the skin, to avoid drying out amphibians must live in or near water or in humid places.

All North American amphibians lay eggs (some amphibians in other parts of the world give birth to living young). The eggs usually hatch into water-dwelling larvae like the familiar tadpole—not resembling the parents at first, although eventually transforming into the adult form. But the eggs of some amphibians hatch as fully transformed young. Among these are the Barking, Greenhouse, Cliff, Foothills, and Rio Grande toads and the Ensatina, woodland, climbing, web-toed, and slender salamanders. But whatever their life history, all amphibians have external gills at some time, whether as larvae, in the egg, or in the uterus. No other limbed vertebrates—mammals, birds, or reptiles—have external gills at any stage of development.

EGGS of amphibians lack shells and usually can be identified as to species only by microscopic examination. Among frogs and toads, only the narrow-toed toads lay eggs on land, but many species of salamanders do so, notably the Marbled Salamander and some of the lungless salamanders. Many salamanders lay their eggs singly in water, in some cases attaching them to the undersides of objects; among frogs and toads, only the Red-spotted Toad and a few species of true treefrogs and chorus frogs lay single eggs. Eggs laid in clumps by salamanders resemble frogs' eggs except that often, particularly among members of the mole salamander family, the entire clump is encased in a jelly envelope. Salamanders never deposit eggs as a surface film; all narrow-mouthed toads, many true frogs, and the Pine Woods Treefrog do so. True toads, the Tailed Toad, spadefoot toads, and quite a few species of salamanders commonly lay eggs in a pair of strings, one from each oviduct.

Among North American frogs and toads, only the Tailed Toad lays white eggs that lack pigment, though many salamanders do so, mostly in shady places on land. Pigmented eggs are laid in water and usually in the sun. The black or brown pigment absorbs the sun's heat, and the eggs develop faster, needing less yolk, and so are smaller than those without pigment. At first pigment occurs only on the upper surface, the lower surface being white or yellow. As the eggs develop, the pigment covers the entire surface.

SALAMANDER

FROG

CAECILIAN

lizard
forefoot has
5 toes

amphibian
forefoot
has 4 toes

egg string
of American
Toad

egg mass of
Wood Frog

egg mass of
Spotted Salamander

FROGS AND TOADS—order Salientia

In the United States and Canada live eight families, 19 genera, 80 species, and 114–116 subspecies of frogs and toads. All are referred to by biologists as anurans (from the superorder name Anura, meaning "without tail"). In this book an arbitrary division is made, restricting the name *frog* to advanced anurans (the treefrogs and true frogs) and using the name *toad* for all others.

Frogs and toads are among the most distinctive of all vertebrates. No other living group of backboned creatures has the adult anuran's particular combination of characteristics: four well-developed limbs, hind limbs modified for jumping, no conspicuous tail, well-developed eyes with lids. Microscopic mucous glands keep the thin skin moist; in most species the skin also contains microscopic poison glands.

The typical life history of a North American frog or toad starts with the egg, laid in water. A female may deposit as few as 19 to as many as 30,000 eggs in one breeding period. Individually encased in thin gelatinous envelopes, the eggs are typically laid in strings or masses underwater or as a film on the water's surface. Eggs hatch into tadpoles in 40 hours to 30 days. Depending on the species, the envelope may disintegrate, freeing the tadpole, or may be dissolved by a secretion from glands on the tadpole's snout.

A newly hatched tadpole has external gills that remove oxygen from the water. The gills are soon covered by the body wall but one or two openings, called spiracles, remain. Water thereafter is taken in at the mouth, passes over the enclosed gills, leaves through the spiracles. The tadpole rapidly acquires a lengthy compressed tail. The round body becomes ovoid. The mouthparts are specialized for scraping algae from objects underwater. The long coiled digestive tract is suitable for the strictly plant diet.

After a period of growth, hind legs appear, the tail is absorbed, mouthparts change, the digestive tract shortens in anticipation of the insect diet to come, forelegs appear, and the transformed froglet or toadlet hops onto land. Tadpoles transform in 12 days to 3 years.

Frogs and toads reach sexual maturity in 1 to 4 years. They breed at the time of spring rains, returning to water if they have left it. Males, often in large choruses, typically call to females at night. The male clasps an attracted female either under the armpits (axillary amplexus) or by the groin (inguinal amplexus) until she has laid all her eggs—which may take several hours. As the laying goes on, the male releases sperm that reach the eggs by chemical attraction and fertilize them.

A few North American toads lay eggs on land. The tadpoles develop in the eggs or find their way to water (see p. 24).

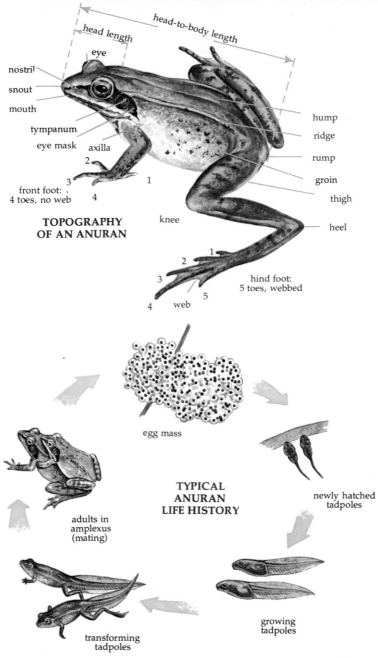

head-to-body length

head length

eye

nostril

snout

mouth

tympanum

eye mask   axilla

2

3

front foot:
4 toes, no web

4

hump

ridge

rump

groin

thigh

heel

1

knee

**TOPOGRAPHY
OF AN ANURAN**

1

2

3

4   web   5

hind foot:
5 toes, webbed

egg mass

**TYPICAL
ANURAN
LIFE HISTORY**

newly hatched
tadpoles

adults in
amplexus
(mating)

growing
tadpoles

transforming
tadpoles

MATING CALLS are sounded during the breeding season by males of most species. (Both sexes of all species are believed capable of producing sound when in distress.) Calls are made by passing air over the vocal cords. Often a vocal sac or a pair of sacs provide resonance. Each species has a distinctive call; thus females can recognize their own males. Human listeners also can identify species of frogs and toads by their calls.

Mating calls may be learned by listening either to recordings or to actual singers in the field, although the latter method generally requires capture of the specimen for positive identification. While calls can be reproduced visually as sonograms, even experts are not able to reliably reconstruct mentally most calls so depicted.

Mating calls for many species are described in this book. It is impossible to "key" such calls in a brief, readily intelligible way, but certain useful generalizations can be made. Most toads produce a trill lasting 0.5–30 seconds. Some chorus frogs utter a short coarse trill, approximated closely by running the thumb over the teeth of a comb from center to tip. Eastern and Western Narrow-mouthed toads emit a faint high-pitched buzz. The Sheep Toad, of course, bleats like a sheep. Cliff and Rio Grande toads chirp like crickets. Treefrogs utter birdlike calls. Spadefoot and Cone-nosed toads make a vomiting noise. The calls of most true frogs are deep and guttural and may sound like snoring.

IDENTIFICATION of frogs and toads requires attention to different clues at each stage of development—egg, tadpole, and adult. Identification may be difficult during the period of transition from one stage to another, because structures pertinent to a given stage may yet be undeveloped or already degenerate. Transformed individuals, for example, are often troublesome to identify until their features mature enough to approximate those of the adult animal. Fortunately, few individuals in a transitional stage are encountered and so, in practice, most frogs and toads can be identified without difficulty.

KEY TO FAMILIES OF ADULT FROGS AND TOADS

1. Pupil of eye vertical when contracted .... *see* **2**
   Pupil horizontal .... *see* **3**
2. Outer hind toe thicker than others; males with short "tails" .... **bell toads,** p. 30
   Neither of above .... *see* **7**
3. Parotoid glands present .... **true toads,** p. 36
   No parotoid glands .... *see* **4**
4. Groove across head behind eyes; no distinguishable tympanum ...**narrow-mouthed toads,** p. 26
   No groove, or if present, tympanum visible .... *see* **5**
5. No webs between toes ....**narrow-toed toads,** p.28
   At least short toe webs .... *see* **6**
6. Intercalary cartilage between last 2 phalanges ......**treefrogs,** p.46
   No cartilage ....**true frogs,** p.60
7. Head much narrower than body .... **cone-nosed toads,** p. 26
   Head slightly narrower than body .....**spadefoot toads,** p. 32

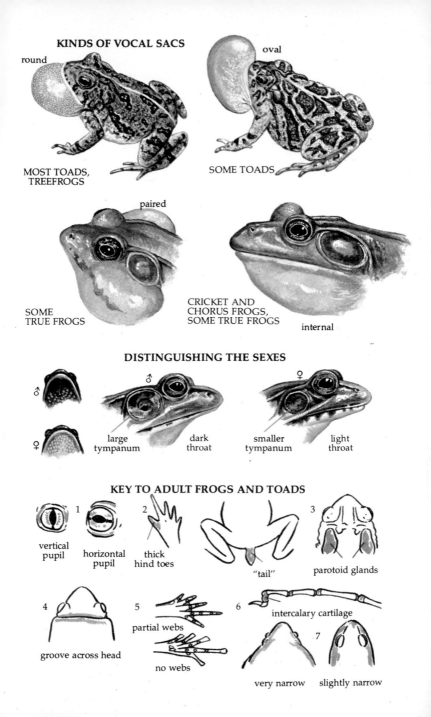

KINDS OF VOCAL SACS

round

oval

MOST TOADS,
TREEFROGS

SOME TOADS

paired

SOME
TRUE FROGS

CRICKET AND
CHORUS FROGS,
SOME TRUE FROGS

internal

DISTINGUISHING THE SEXES

♂

♀

♂

large
tympanum

dark
throat

♀

smaller
tympanum

light
throat

KEY TO ADULT FROGS AND TOADS

1

vertical
pupil

horizontal
pupil

2

thick
hind toes

"tail"

3

parotoid glands

4

groove across head

5

partial webs

no webs

6

intercalary cartilage

7

very narrow   slightly narrow

TADPOLES are identified partly by number and position of the spiracles and position of the vent but mostly by the mouthparts. Tadpoles of the Tailed Toad have a greatly enlarged mouth disc used for adhesion to rocks in swift-flowing streams. Tadpoles of the narrow-mouthed toads (family Microhylidae) have a very small mouth disc that lacks rasping structures. Variations in the mouthparts of other tadpoles are less apparent. Because the mouthparts are immature during early development and degenerate during later development, identification may be difficult or even impossible. But during the middle period of development, all tadpoles—except some members of the treefrog family (Hylidae)—are easily identified at least to the genus level, as indicated in the key below. Geographic origin will then usually indicate species or limit the possibilities to only a few species.

The key does not include the Greenhouse, Barking, Cliff, and Rio Grande toads because they produce no free-living tadpoles. The tadpoles of those species develop in the eggs, which are laid on land and hatch into transformed toadlets. A more complete key to species is given by R. Altig in *Herpetologica*, vol. 26, 1970, pp. 180–207.

KEY TO TADPOLES

1. Horny black mouth structures ....*see* **4**
   No such structures .... *see* **2**
2. Spiracle on each side of body ....**Cone-nosed Toad,** p. 26
   Spiracle at middle rear of underside ....*see* **3**
3. Edge of labial flaps scalloped or papillate ......**Sheep Toad,** p. 26
   Edge of labial flaps smooth ....**narrow-mouthed toads,** p. 26
4. Spiracle at middle front of underside ....**Tailed Toad,** p. 30
   Spiracle on left side only ......*see* **5**
5. Vent in middle ....*see* **6**
   Vent at right ....*see* **9**
6. Both upper and lower papillary fringes incomplete in middle ... .**true toads,** p. 36
   Lower fringe complete, upper complete or not ....*see* **7**
7. 3 rows of spicules on lower oral disc ....**Greenhouse** or **White-lipped Toad,** pp. 28, 30
   4 rows ....*see* **8**
8. Jaws wide, often cusped, never striated ....
   Western, Great Basin, or **Plains Spadefoot,** pp.32, 34

   Jaws narrow, never cusped; lower jaw striated ....**Eastern** or **Couch's Spadefoot,** p. 34
9. Oral disc deeply indented on each side of mouth.................*see* **10**
   Disc not so indented ....*see* **13**
10. 2 rows of spicules on lower oral disc ....*see* **11**
    3 or 4 rows ....*see* **12**
11. Bottom row of spicules in upper disc widely interrupted ....**Northern** and **Southern Cricket Frogs,** p. 48
    Bottom row narrowly interrupted ....**Least Grassfrog,** p. 48; **Northern Chorus Frog** and **Peeper Treefrog,** p. 52, 56
12. *(not shown)* 4 rows of spicules on lower part of oral disc ....**Cuban Treefrog,** p. 58
    3 rows of spicules ....**other treefrogs,** p. 46
13. Lower part of papillary fringe widely interrupted in middle ....**true toads,** p. 36
    Lower part complete ....**true frogs,** p. 60

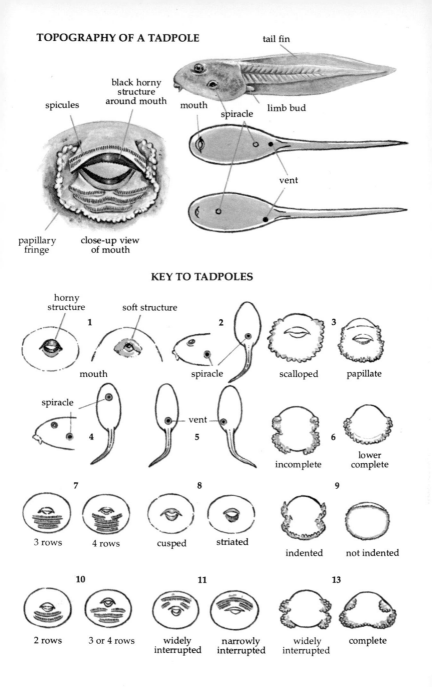

TOPOGRAPHY OF A TADPOLE

tail fin

black horny structure around mouth

spicules

mouth

spiracle

limb bud

vent

papillary fringe

close-up view of mouth

KEY TO TADPOLES

horny structure

soft structure

1

mouth

2

spiracle

3

scalloped

papillate

spiracle

4

5

vent

6

incomplete

lower complete

7

3 rows

4 rows

8

cusped

striated

9

indented

not indented

10

2 rows

3 or 4 rows

11

widely interrupted

narrowly interrupted

13

widely interrupted

complete

CONE-NOSED TOADS—family Rhinophrynidae

The single living species in this family is a bizarre toad confined largely to Mexico. It was first seen in southern Texas in 1966.

 **CONE-NOSED TOAD** (*Rhinophrynus dorsalis*). Bulbous and flabby body, small pointed head, 2 tubercles at heel. Only N.A. species with tongue attached at rear of mouth. Dark back bears vertebral stripe, yellow to tomato red; belly is uniform gray. This burrowing toad is seldom seen except after rains. Mating call a deep moan.

NARROW-MOUTHED TOADS—family Microhylidae

These smooth-skinned toads are characterized by a swollen-looking body, short fat limbs, a narrow head with pointed snout, a skin fold crossing the rear of head, the presence of heel tubercles. Narrow-mouthed species rarely live near human habitation, are seldom seen except when congregating in pools to breed. Strong burrowers, they emerge only at night and specialize in eating ants. Eggs float on the water surface in a thin film. Tadpoles are distinguished by a soft mouth disc instead of horny jaws and a single spiracle (opening of internal gill chamber) in middle rear of belly rather than on left side as is more common.

 EASTERN NARROW-MOUTHED TOAD (*Gastrophryne carolinensis*). Small, smooth-skinned, short-legged. Gray to brownish or reddish back shows fine dark reticulations or a **V**-shaped dark band with apex near head. Belly is dark-marked. Mating call a buzzing trill of low volume, generally 1–3 seconds.

 WESTERN NARROW-MOUTHED TOAD (*Gastrophryne olivacea*). Similar in body form to Eastern, but grayish, slate, or olive, and never has dark **V** on back or marks on belly. Mating call is a faint buzz of 2–2.5 seconds, preceded by a short squeak. Two subspecies: (1) *G. o. olivacea*—few or no dark spots on hind legs and back; (2) *G. o. mazatlanensis*—distinct dark spots scattered on back and forming bar across thigh and shank.

 SHEEP TOAD (*Hypopachus variolosus*). Bulky body with a smooth skin of rich brown; thin white or yellow line down middle of back and belly; dark triangle on back, apex forward. Has 2 tubercles under heel. Mating call is a loud 2-second bleat, like that of a sheep; every 15–20 seconds. No subspecies recognized at present.

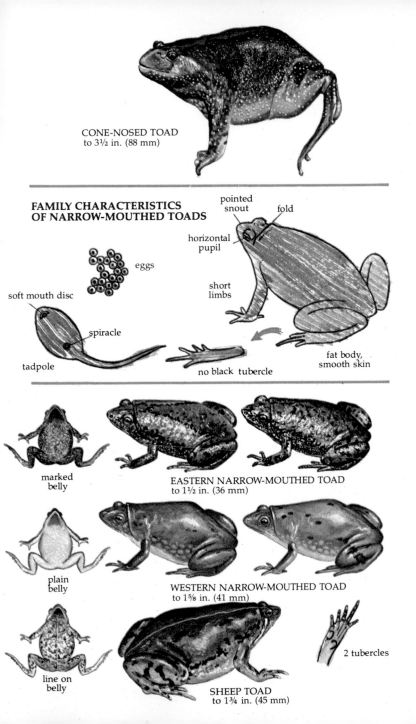

CONE-NOSED TOAD
to 3½ in. (88 mm)

FAMILY CHARACTERISTICS OF NARROW-MOUTHED TOADS

eggs

pointed snout

fold

horizontal pupil

short limbs

soft mouth disc

spiracle

tadpole

no black tubercle

fat body, smooth skin

marked belly

EASTERN NARROW-MOUTHED TOAD
to 1½ in. (36 mm)

plain belly

WESTERN NARROW-MOUTHED TOAD
to 1⅝ in. (41 mm)

line on belly

SHEEP TOAD
to 1¾ in. (45 mm)

2 tubercles

NARROW-TOED TOADS—family Leptodactylidae

These are the only North American toads or frogs that completely lack webs between the toes—thus "narrow-toed." They are also unique in possessing what appears to be, but is not, a suckerlike disc over the entire abdomen. This family lays eggs on land rather than in water. Eggs of all but the White-lipped Toad hatch into land-dwelling toadlets. The White-lipped Toad lays its eggs near temporary pools at the beginning of the rainy season and with its hind legs beats the gelatinous mass enveloping the eggs into a froth. When developed, the tadpoles wriggle through the froth to water.

KEY TO NARROW-TOED TOADS

1. Whitish streak along upper lip ....**White-lipped**, p. 30
   No such streak ....*see* **2**
2. Skin fold on each side of back ....**Barking**, p. 30
   No skin fold on back ....*see* **3**
3. *(not shown)* Reddish ....**Greenhouse**, below
   Not reddish ....*see* **4**

4. Bar between eyes; toes blunt ....**Foothills**, below
   No bar between eyes............*see* **5**
5. Irregular lines or blotches on back; toes blunt .....**Cliff**, below
   Some dots on back; toes rounded ....**Rio Grande**, below

CLIFF TOAD (*Syrrhophus marnocki***).** Smooth skin without folds; greenish, mottled by dark brown. Tympanum as large as eye. Lives in rocky canyons and on ledges of cliffs. Breeds during rainy periods except in midwinter. Mating call like the sound of a cricket.

RIO GRANDE TOAD (*Syrrhophus cystignathoides***).** Similar to Cliff, but smaller and gray-brown with fine dark stippling. Mating call like Cliff's, given irregularly. U.S. subspecies: *S. c. campi.*

FOOTHILLS TOAD (*Syrrhophus guttilatus***).** Similar to Cliff but yellowish to brownish. Dark and light bar between eyes; network of dark spots on the back. Mating call a short shrill note.

GREENHOUSE TOAD (*Eleutherodactylus planirostris***).** Markings vary. Chiefly striped or mottled, with reddish mark on snout, reddish tones on trunk and limbs. Tiny disc terminates each digit. Found under litter in moist places, often in greenhouses. Mating call a series of 4–6 warbling chirps. U.S. subspecies: *E. p. planirostris,* in Florida.

COQUI (*Eleutherodactylus coqui***).** Wide digit tips, bar between eyes. Introduced in Miami, Florida, in 1972. Named after its call: *coqui, coqui.* [Not illustrated; no range map.]

FAMILY CHARACTERISTICS OF NARROW-TOED TOADS

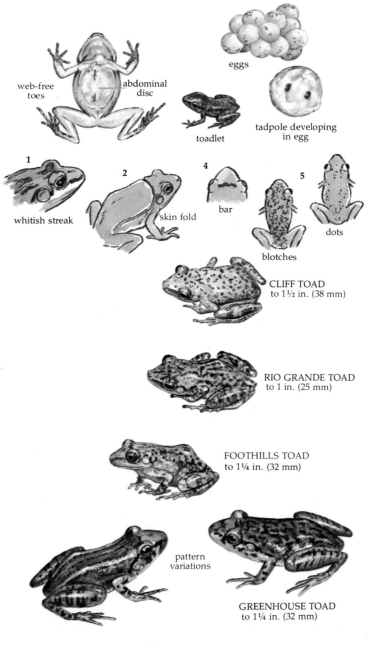

web-free toes

abdominal disc

eggs

toadlet

tadpole developing in egg

1 whitish streak

2 skin fold

4 bar

blotches

5 dots

CLIFF TOAD
to 1½ in. (38 mm)

RIO GRANDE TOAD
to 1 in. (25 mm)

FOOTHILLS TOAD
to 1¼ in. (32 mm)

pattern variations

GREENHOUSE TOAD
to 1¼ in. (32 mm)

WHITE-LIPPED TOAD (*Leptodactylus labialis*). Slate gray to chocolate above, with scattered dark marks. Whitish line along upper lip, dark line through eye. Tympanum is conspicuous; a fold runs over it. Unique among N.A. frogs and toads in that 1st front toe is longer than 2nd by length of last phalanx. Male has a pair of folds in skin of throat and a long shovel-like snout. Lives in moist lowlands near water in savannas or sparse woods. Mating call a short whistled *whoot* or *wheet* uttered once a second.

BARKING TOAD (*Hylactophryne augusti*). Broad head, smooth skin without warts. Skin fold between tympana, also along each side of back. Color brownish or slate with irregular dark mottling. Pale crossband conspicuous in young, barely visible in adults. Digit tips slightly swollen. Inflates to spectacular size when threatened. Secretions are irritating to human eyes and cuts. Secretive and solitary even during spring breeding season; inhabits rocky limestone areas. Mating call is a sharp doglike bark—thus the name—repeated at long intervals. Two subspecies: (1) *H. a. cactorum*—dark gray above; (2) *H. a. latrans*—light brown above.

BELL TOADS—family Leiopelmatidae

This family, which includes the most primitive of all living frogs and toads, is represented in North America by only one species.

TAILED TOAD (*Ascaphus truei*). So named because males have a short "tail"—actually a copulatory organ. Sole N.A. anuran whose eggs are fertilized internally. Skin smooth, but with few to many warts, somewhat more granular in parotoid region. Olive to brown, reddish gray or gray above, with yellow to green triangle on top of snout, dark band between eyes, and dark stripe through eye to shoulder. Pupil is vertical when contracted. Outer rear toe is thicker than others. Front toes not webbed, hind toes one-fourth webbed. Sole of front foot has 3 pads. Lives in or near cold streams, usually in forests; 0–6,500 feet. Breeds in early fall, female carrying sperm until eggs are laid, May to September, hatching in a month; larvae overwinter once or twice. At high altitudes, females breed in alternate years. No mating call.

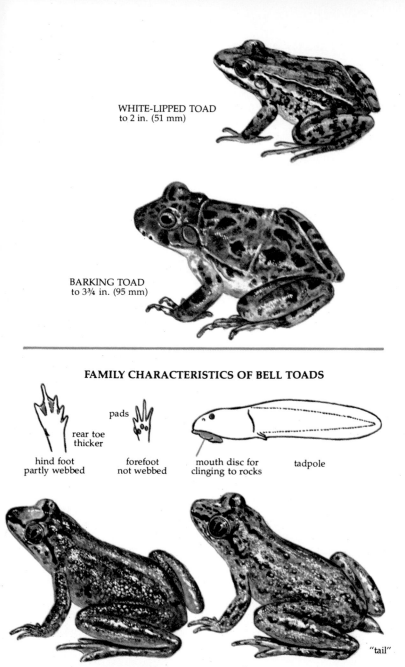

WHITE-LIPPED TOAD
to 2 in. (51 mm)

BARKING TOAD
to 3¾ in. (95 mm)

FAMILY CHARACTERISTICS OF BELL TOADS

rear toe
thicker

hind foot
partly webbed

pads

forefoot
not webbed

mouth disc for
clinging to rocks

tadpole

TAILED TOAD
to 2 in. (51 mm)

"tail"

31

SPADEFOOT TOADS—family Pelobatidae

These plump toads have two distinguishing characteristics: (1) eye pupil is vertical when it contracts in bright light—in all other North American frogs and toads except Tailed and Cone-nosed, contracted pupil is horizontal; (2) inner side of each hind foot has a conspicuous black horny "spade," a feature shared only with Cone-nosed and a few true toads. Spadefoots burrow into sandy soil by shuffling hind feet like spades to scoop away soil as the toad spirals backward out of sight. Nocturnal creatures, they emerge during darkness to feed, especially when soil is damp, but may not come out at all in periods of drought. Skin is warty to varying degrees but rather smooth between warts. Tips of toes are sometimes black. The male has a darker throat than the female and dark horny patches on inner edge of first, and sometimes second and third front toes.

Spadefoot toads breed after the first heavy rains following winter. If rains come late, they breed late; if no heavy rains fall during the year, they do not breed. Males select shallow temporary pools for breeding, and their loud calls at night attract spadefoots from miles away. Since the pools often dry up quickly, the development periods of spadefoot eggs and tadpoles are the shortest of any known frog or toad; transformation to land-dwelling subadults occurs in as few as 12–13 days if circumstances demand it. If food is scarce or conditions crowded, tadpoles may become cannibalistic and reach relatively enormous size before transforming. All spadefoot species have a large tongue.

KEY TO SPADEFOOT TOADS

1. Short, rounded spade on rear foot..............................*see* **2**
   Sickle-shaped spade ....*see* **4**
2. Boss (hump) between eyes....*see* **3**
   No boss..............**Western,** below
3. High boss between eyes, extending forward ....**Plains,** p. 34
   Low boss, not extending forward ....**Great Basin,** p. 34
4. Dark edge of spade at least 3 times longer than wide ....
   ....**Eastern,** p. 34
   Dark edge of spade no more than 2 times longer than wide ....
   ....**Couch's,** p. 34

WESTERN SPADEFOOT (*Spea hammondi*). Only spadefoot of western states with no boss (hump) between eyes. Greenish, gray, or brown with dark markings, often four faint pale streaks. Small tubercles, sometimes with reddish or yellow tips above, white below. Short rounded spade on hind foot, slightly webbed front toes, nearly fully webbed hind toes. Lives chiefly in moist lowlands, also in moderately dry areas. Mating call a raspy snoring sound lasting 0.5–1.25 seconds. Two subspecies: (1) *S. h. hammondi*—call less than 1 second; (2) *S.h. multiplicata*—call longer than 1 second.

FAMILY CHARACTERISTICS OF SPADEFOOT TOADS

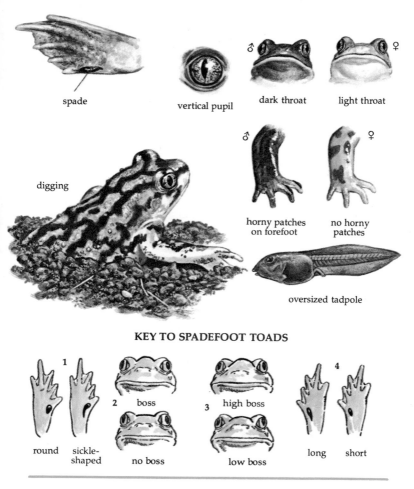

spade

vertical pupil

♂ dark throat

♀ light throat

digging

♂ horny patches on forefoot

♀ no horny patches

oversized tadpole

KEY TO SPADEFOOT TOADS

1 round   sickle-shaped

2 boss   no boss

3 high boss   low boss

4 long   short

WESTERN SPADEFOOT TOAD
to 2⅝ in. (68 mm)

GREAT BASIN SPADEFOOT (*Spea intermontana*). Much like Western (p. 32) in form except for a low boss between the eyes, located not so far forward as in Plains. This hump is mostly thickened skin and thus rather soft. Tubercles have no reddish tips, are more numerous, smaller, and more variable in size than in Western. Ecological range is broader, extending from low sagebrush to spruce-fir level. Mating call a rapid series of rasping squawks, each lasting 0.2–0.3 second.

PLAINS SPADEFOOT (*Spea bombifrons*). Also resembles Western (p. 32) but has high bony boss between eyes—higher, farther forward, and harder than in Great Basin. Tubercles are larger and more prominent, often with reddish or yellowish tips, back is pale gray or brownish rather than greenish with dimly evident pale streaks. Belly is white. Spade on hind foot is short and rounded. Front toes are slightly webbed, hind toes nearly fully webbed. Plains Spadefoots are abundant in sandy areas. Mating call a sharp quack lasting about 0.2–0.7 second.

COUCH'S SPADEFOOT (*Scaphiopus couchi*). This species differs from Plains in having sickle-shaped spades, eyes wider apart, webless front toes, fully webbed hind toes. Color is a greenish- or brownish-yellow, with black, dark brown, or dark green markings, often reticular in western individuals and irregularly blotched in eastern individuals. Inhabits relatively dry plains and semidesert. Mating call a bleat lasting 1.3–2.5 seconds.

EASTERN SPADEFOOT (*Scaphiopus holbrooki*). Usually has a pair of sinuous pale lines extending rearward from eyes, sometimes a less evident pale line along each side. Only spadefoot found E of the Mississippi; only one with a distinct tympanum. Like Couch's, the Eastern has sickle-shaped spades and eyes wider apart than in other species. Front toes slightly webbed, hind toes nearly fully webbed. Back is gray or brown to black, often tinged with green; belly white. Mating call an explosive nasal *quonk* repeated several times a minute. Two subspecies: (1) *S. h. holbrooki*—no boss between eyes; (2) *S. h. hurteri*—boss between eyes.

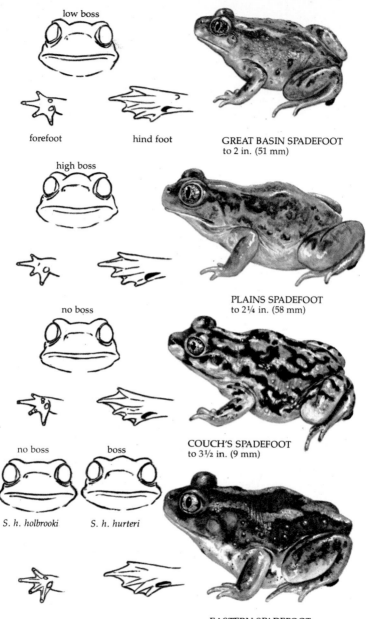

low boss

forefoot   hind foot

GREAT BASIN SPADEFOOT
to 2 in. (51 mm)

high boss

PLAINS SPADEFOOT
to 2¼ in. (58 mm)

no boss

COUCH'S SPADEFOOT
to 3½ in. (9 mm)

no boss   boss

S. h. holbrooki   *S. h. hurteri*

EASTERN SPADEFOOT
to 3½ in. (90 mm)

TRUE TOADS—family Bufonidae

Of the 19 genera and some 277 species of true toads in the world, only one genus (*Bufo*), comprising 17 species, lives in North America north of Mexico. The species range in size from the Oak Toad (p. 42), about 1.3 inches long, to the Marine Toad (p. 44), which may reach 9 inches.

The most obvious characteristic of true toads is their extremely warty skin. Each wart is a clump of swollen poison glands, as are the large parotoid glands on either side of the neck. The poison is powerful enough to sicken or kill dogs, snakes, and other predators that take toads into their mouths. Even humans have died from eating the highly poisonous Marine Toad. Toads do not, however, cause warts in people.

Most toads and frogs have upper but not lower teeth; true toads have no teeth at all. Toothed or not, toads will try to eat almost any moving object small enough to swallow—but seldom their young. They judge some insects distasteful and spit them out immediately. For most species of true toads, the normal method of locomotion is hopping, but a few species generally run or walk.

Though common in many places, true toads are seldom seen in abundance except during the breeding season. Large numbers then congregate in shallow, often temporary pools, and the mating calls of the male chorus may be audible for a mile. A vocal sac serves as a resonator for the trills and is inflated to various shapes according to the species.

Males use their front limbs to clasp attracted females. Since males cannot distinguish sex by sight, a male sometimes clasps another male by mistake but releases it upon hearing a croak of objection. A male may cling to a female for days until she lays her eggs, typically in a pair of gelatinous strings. The female usually walks around while laying, so the strings become tangled together over a large area. No four-footed animal lays more eggs than the true toad—in the Marine Toad, as many as 30,000 in a single clutch; in the common American Toad, as many as 25,000.

When the breeding season is over, true toads, their mating calls silenced, scatter far and wide. Since they are among the most resistant of all frogs and toads to dehydration, true toads are usually not restricted to the immediate vicinity of water. They cannot wander far, however, from moist places. Often a true toad will stay for weeks or months in a particular cool, damp, protected spot, emerging only at night to seek food. Some species are abundant even near houses, hiding by day under steps, boards, or debris. These toads often learn to wait under outdoor lights on spring and summer nights for the insects attracted by the illumination. Other species seldom occur near human habitations. These more timid toads commonly spend the day in burrows or ground crevices, or among damp rocks.

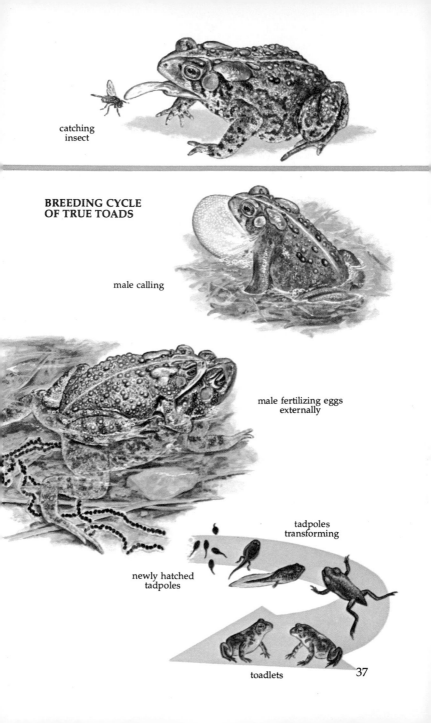

catching
insect

**BREEDING CYCLE
OF TRUE TOADS**

male calling

male fertilizing eggs
externally

tadpoles
transforming

newly hatched
tadpoles

toadlets

37

IDENTIFICATION of true toads is based largely on the prominence, size, and shape of cranial crests (the bony ridges on the head), parotoid glands, and warts. Other characteristics useful for identification are color and pattern, the presence or absence of a boss (hump) between the eyes, and the sharpness of tubercles (lumps) on the underside of the hind feet. Immature individuals are difficult to identify because of the slow development of adult features, especially the cranial crests. Males are usually smaller and sometimes have a darker throat than females. Only males possess a vocal sac, which they inflate when calling. The inner surface of the male's first (inner) front toe is roughened by a thick black or dark brown layer of horny material, a feature that helps him clasp the female while mating.

KEY TO TRUE TOADS

1. Parotoid glands round or transversely oval..**Red-spotted,** p. 40
   Parotoid glands elongate ......*see* **2**
2. Parotoid glands as long as head, extending lower than tympanum ....*see* **3**
   Parotoid glands not as long as head, not extending lower than tympanum ....*see* **5**
3. (*not shown*) Brownish, to 9 in. ....**Marine,** p. 44
   Greenish with black markings, to 2¼ in. ....*see* **4**
4. Black marks small, separated ....**Plains Green,** p. 44
   Black marks forming continuous network ..**Sonoran Green,** p. 44
5. (*not shown*) No large warts except on hind legs ....
   ....**Colorado River,** p. 44
   Profusely warty ....*see* **6**
6. Cranial crests unite somewhere along their length, forming a boss ....*see* **7**
   No large boss ....*see* **8**
7. Boss at front border of eyes only ....**Great Plains,** p. 44
   Boss at rear border of eyes or throughout their length ....
   ....**Dakota,** p. 42
8. Maximum length 1¼ in.; orange to white stripe down middle of back ....**Oak,** p. 42
   Much larger (minimum breeding length about 1¾ in.); back stripe present or not ....*see* **9**

9. Cranial crests faint or absent ....
   ....*see* **10**
   Cranial crests distinct ....*see* **13**
10. Sharp edge on inner tubercle on sole of hind foot ....*see* **11**
    No sharp edge on inner tubercle on hind foot ....*see* **12**
11. Light bar across top of head at eyelid level ....
    ....**Southwestern,** p. 40
    No light bar ....**Texas,** p. 40
12. Parotoid glands rather diffuse, each wider than the distance between them ..**Yosemite,** p. 40
    Parotoid glands sharply defined, each narrower than distance between them ...**Western,** p. 40
13. Parotoid glands nearly triangular ....**Gulf Coast,** p. 44
    Parotoid glands elongate. ....*see* **14**
14. Rear of cranial crests swollen, knoblike ....**Southern,** p.42
    Cranial crests not knoblike ..*see* **15**
15. Cranial crests thickened, especially back of eyes; back dark mottled ....**Houston,** p. 42
    Cranial crests not thickened, back not mottled ....*see* **16**
16. Parotoid glands separated from crest or connected to it by short spur ......**American,** p. 42
    Parotoid glands touch crest, no spur ....**Common,** p. 42

FAMILY CHARACTERISTICS OF TRUE TOADS

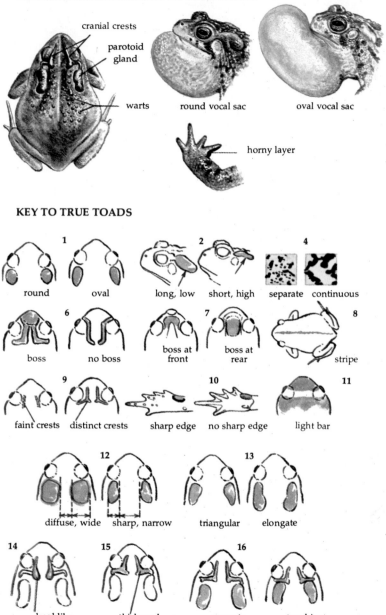

cranial crests

parotoid gland

warts

round vocal sac

oval vocal sac

horny layer

KEY TO TRUE TOADS

1
round — oval

2
long, low — short, high

4
separate — continuous

6
boss — no boss

7
boss at front — boss at rear

8
stripe

9
faint crests — distinct crests

10
sharp edge — no sharp edge

11
light bar

12
diffuse, wide — sharp, narrow

13
triangular — elongate

14
knoblike

15
thickened

16
separate — touching

39

WESTERN TOAD (*Bufo boreas*). Has oval parotoid glands about size of upper eyelid, an almost equally large gland on shank. Brownish to greenish, spotted irregularly above and below, with pale line on back except in young. Four subspecies: (1) *B. b. boreas*—fairly dark; (2) *B. b. exsul*—very dark, to 2.4 inches, skin smooth between warts; (3) *B. b. halophilus*—greenish, pale bellied; (4) *B. b. nelsoni*—long-bodied (elbow and knee do not touch when appressed). First subspecies has no mating call, others probably not; all chirp like chicks when disturbed.

YOSEMITE TOAD (*Bufo canorus*). Parotoid glands wider, flatter, and closer together than in Western Toad. Narrow light line on back, spotted belly, large warts, smooth skin. Color yellow-olive to olive-black above; females and young brightly spotted. Mating call a pleasant vibrato of 10–20 notes, repeated often.

SOUTHWESTERN TOAD (*Bufo microscaphus*). Oval parotoid glands twice as long as wide. Small, often red-tipped warts. Pale bar across eyes. Back is greenish, reddish, or brownish, with or without dark spots and faint light-colored line; belly whitish. Throat dark in males. Mating call a trill of 8–10 seconds. Two subspecies: (1) *B. m. microscaphus*—skin relatively smooth, dark spots faint or absent; (2) *B. m. californicus*—skin relatively rough, dark spots prominent.

RED-SPOTTED TOAD (*Bufo punctatus*). Round or slightly oval (transversely) parotoid glands. Head and body conspicuously flattened, pointed snout. Color varies from pearl gray to brownish red above, sometimes with small spots. Warts usually brightly tipped with yellow, orange, or red. Belly all white or with dark flecks. Throat dark in males. Mating call a high-pitched trill of 6–10 seconds.

TEXAS TOAD (*Bufo speciosus*). Has short oval parotoid glands, less than twice as long as wide. Many uniformly small warts; 2 black tubercles with free digging edges on sole of rear foot. Color is greenish gray to brown above with small scattered irregular dark spots; belly unspotted; crests low. Mating call a shrill trill lasting 0.5–1 second, repeated at intervals of the same length.

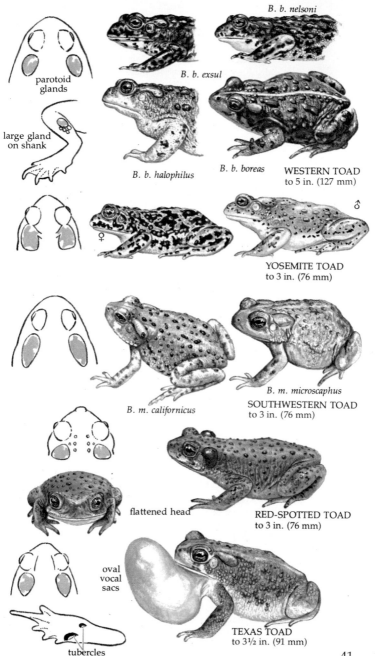

parotoid glands

large gland on shank

B. b. nelsoni

B. b. exsul

B. b. halophilus

B. b. boreas

WESTERN TOAD
to 5 in. (127 mm)

♀

♂

YOSEMITE TOAD
to 3 in. (76 mm)

B. m. californicus

B. m. microscaphus

SOUTHWESTERN TOAD
to 3 in. (76 mm)

flattened head

RED-SPOTTED TOAD
to 3 in. (76 mm)

oval vocal sacs

tubercles

TEXAS TOAD
to 3½ in. (91 mm)

AMERICAN TOAD (*Bufo americanus*). Common in eastern N.A. Parotoid glands are 2–3 times as long as wide, do not touch cranial crests unless by a short spur. Color usually brownish but varies; male's throat is black. Mating call a melodious trill of 6–30 seconds. Three subspecies: (1) *B. a. americanus*—large wart on each dark spot on back; (2) *B. a. copei*—several warts per dark spot, vivid markings (especially below); (3) *B. a. charlesmithi*—smaller, usually unspotted, may be red-hued above.

OAK TOAD (*Bufo quercicus*). Smallest true toad in N.A. Parotoids large and oval, extending lower than tympanum. Prominent pale line down back, straddled by 4–5 pairs of dark spots. Cranial crests low. Color and pattern variable; belly shows scant to dense dark flecking. Mating call like a chick's chirp.

SOUTHERN TOAD (*Bufo terrestris*). Distinguishable by knoblike swellings at rear of cranial crests (less evident in young). Parotoid glands about twice as long as wide, do not touch crests. Dark spots on back may extend over warts. Belly pale, unmarked. Male's throat dark. Mating call a high rapid trill, 2–8 seconds.

COMMON OR WOODHOUSE'S TOAD (*Bufo woodhousei*). Parotoids about twice as long as wide, touch crests. Pale line down back. Color varies; male's throat dark. Mating call, 1–4 seconds, a dissonant trill-like bleat. Four subspecies: (1) *B. w. woodhousei*—pale line to snout, belly with few flecks or none; (2) *B. w. australis*—line not to snout, chest black-marked at sides; (3) *B. w. fowleri*—like (1) but smaller, with large black spots each containing 3–4 warts; (4) *B. w. velatus*—dark-chested.

HOUSTON TOAD (*Bufo houstonensis*). Parotoids, thick cranial crests, warts as in American. Dark-dotted belly, and usually a pale line on back. Male's throat dark. Mating call a shrill liquid trill of 4–11 seconds. Rare and endangered.

DAKOTA TOAD (*Bufo hemiophrys*). Cranial crests fused into long boss; parotoids and warts as in American. Pale line down back; male's throat dark. Mating call a deep muted vibrato of 1.5–5 seconds, given every 30 seconds. Two subspecies: (1) *B. h. hemiophrys*—wider pale line on back; (2) *B. h. baxteri*—narrower pale line.

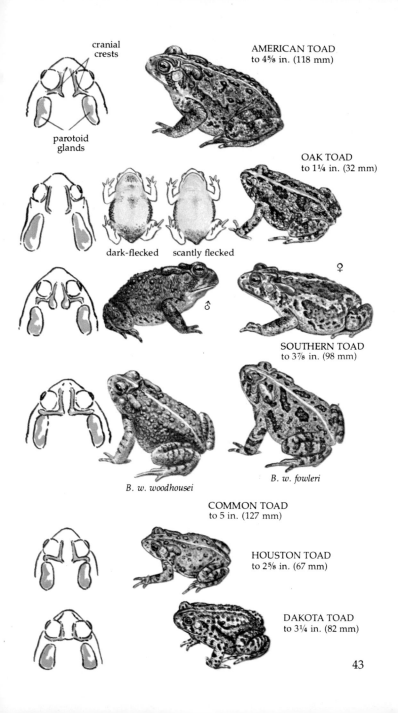

cranial crests

parotoid glands

AMERICAN TOAD
to 4⅝ in. (118 mm)

OAK TOAD
to 1¼ in. (32 mm)

dark-flecked   scantly flecked

♂   ♀

SOUTHERN TOAD
to 3⅞ in. (98 mm)

B. w. woodhousei   *B. w. fowleri*

COMMON TOAD
to 5 in. (127 mm)

HOUSTON TOAD
to 2⅝ in. (67 mm)

DAKOTA TOAD
to 3¼ in. (82 mm)

43

PLAINS GREEN TOAD (*Bufo debilis*). Large subtriangular parotoids, low cranial crests. Green to greenish yellow above, with black flecks; some warts tipped with orange or yellow. Mating call a faint trill of 2–7 seconds, repeated after 5 seconds. Two subspecies: (1) *B. d. debilis*—crests smooth in front of and below eyes; (2) *B. d. insidior*—crests bumpy near eyes.

SONORAN GREEN TOAD (*Bufo retiformis*). Basically like Plains Green but has closed black network above, with eye-sized or larger meshes in which green appears. Mating call a faint but piercing trill of 1–3 seconds.

MARINE TOAD (*Bufo marinus*). The largest toad. Enormous pocked parotoid glands reach to level of mouth. Cranial crests wide apart, head somewhat concave between. Warts large but low. Pattern varies from brightly mottled to uniform dull brown above. Belly unspotted. Mating call a deep sluggish trill. U.S. subspecies: *B. m. horribilis.*

COLORADO RIVER TOAD (*Bufo alvarius*). Quite large. Long parotoid glands touch cranial crests and extend diagonally downward. Brown to gray or olive. Smooth-skinned, with scattered small warts on back and several large ones on hind legs. Warts are rimmed with black in young. At or behind corner of mouth is a white streak or fleck. Skin poison notably potent. Mating call a deep, low-volume *honk* of 0.5–1 second.

GULF COAST TOAD (*Bufo valliceps*). Parotoid glands almost triangular; cranial crests high, far apart. Has row of warts along each side, with pale stripe above and dark stripe below. Color above ranges from nearly black with orange spots to brown with white spots. Belly may be either unmarked or stippled, often darkly blotched in young. Mating call a clattering trill of 2–6 seconds uttered at intervals of 1–4 seconds. U.S. subspecies: *B. v. valliceps.*

GREAT PLAINS TOAD (*Bufo cognatus*). Cranial crests join at boss on snout; oval parotoid glands touch crests behind eyes, extend diagonally downward. Has large light-edged dark spots on back, unspotted belly. Warts are small, uniform. Males have dark throat. Mating call a high-pitched metallic vibrato of 5–50 seconds.

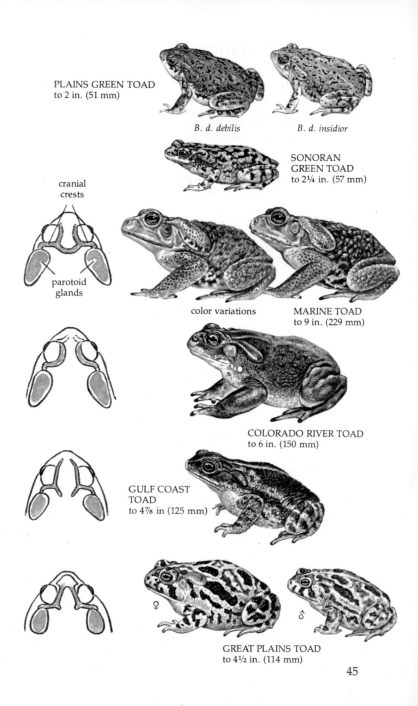

PLAINS GREEN TOAD
to 2 in. (51 mm)

B. d. debilis

B. d. insidior

SONORAN
GREEN TOAD
to 2¼ in. (57 mm)

cranial
crests

parotoid
glands

color variations

MARINE TOAD
to 9 in. (229 mm)

COLORADO RIVER TOAD
to 6 in. (150 mm)

GULF COAST
TOAD
to 4⅞ in (125 mm)

♀

♂

GREAT PLAINS TOAD
to 4½ in. (114 mm)

45

TREEFROGS—family Hylidae

Most treefrogs are small and slim, have long slender legs. Despite their name, they are not all tree-climbers. Their ancestors were adapted for tree-climbing by an enlarged adhesive pad at the tip of each toe. These pads have been retained by the true treefrogs (p. 54). In the course of evolution, other hylid species lost or almost lost the pads and reverted to terrestrial habits. Those species, if they climb at all, climb only low-growing plants. All North American treefrogs, however, have retained a short extra cartilage between the pad and the rest of the digit. In treefrogs that have pads, this intercalary cartilage serves partly as a mechanical aid to muscles lifting the pads, partly as a swivel allowing flat placement of the pads on surfaces. The pads also cushion the abrupt "take-off" stress when a treefrog jumps. Families of treefrogs outside North America that have comparable pads but no intercalary cartilage are not good climbers and stay mostly on the ground or in low shrubs.

The life history of members of the treefrog family is the typical one of other North American anurans (p. 20). Many have flash colors on the hind legs and sides of the body. These colors, which are thought to catch the eye of a predator when the frog leaps, disappear from view when the frog lands and folds his legs, thus causing the predator to lose sight of its prey. The treefrog species vary greatly in color. Some even change color as background color changes.

Most males have paired or single vocal pouches that swell during the call to females. In some species the pouches puff out on either side at the rear of the head. Other species have no sacs and seemingly no voice. Most males also have on the inner side of each front foot, depending on the species, either a corneous pad or horny spines that aid in clasping the female during mating.

KEY TO TREEFROGS

1. Slight webbing on rear foot, a fourth or less length of digits ....*see* **2**
   Extensive webbing on rear foot, at least half length of digits ....*see* **4**
2. Dark lines on sides; no teeth on palate (*use hand lens*); body not over ¾ in. long ....**Least Grassfrog,** p. 48
   No dark line; teeth present on palate; body more than ¾ in. long ....*see* **3**
3. Low skin fold across back of head ....**Burrowing Treefrog,** p. 48
   No skin fold across head ....**chorus frogs,** p. 50

4. Round pads on digit tips ......*see* **5**
   No round pads on digit tips ..*see* **6**
5. Tympanum nearly eye size; paired vocal sacs in males ....**Mexican Smilisca,** p. 48
   Tympanum three-fourths eye size or less; single vocal sac in males ....**true treefrogs,** p. 54
6. Sharp-edged dark stripe on rear of thigh ....**Southern Cricket,** p. 48
   Fuzzy dark stripe on rear of thigh ....**Northern Cricket,** p. 48

46

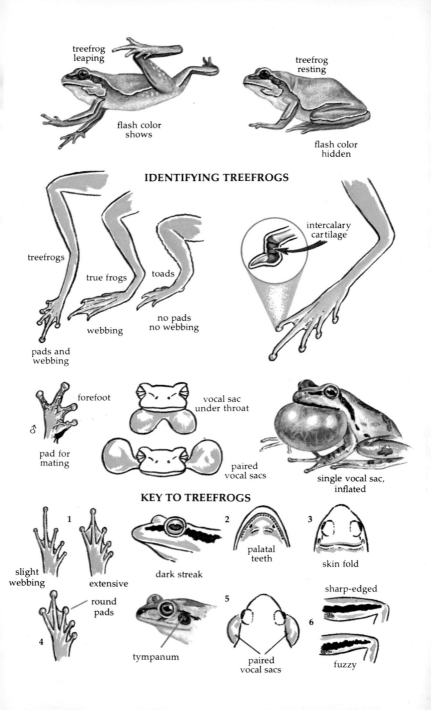

treefrog leaping

flash color shows

treefrog resting

flash color hidden

IDENTIFYING TREEFROGS

intercalary cartilage

treefrogs

true frogs

toads

webbing

no pads no webbing

pads and webbing

forefoot

♂

pad for mating

vocal sac under throat

paired vocal sacs

single vocal sac, inflated

KEY TO TREEFROGS

1

slight webbing

extensive

dark streak

2

palatal teeth

3

skin fold

4

round pads

tympanum

5

paired vocal sacs

sharp-edged

6

fuzzy

LEAST GRASSFROG (*Limnaoedus ocularis*). This is the smallest N.A. frog. Yellowish to greenish or reddish, usually with dark line on side of head and body. Toe pads are tiny. Males have single vocal sac. Mating call a series of scarcely audible chirps, extremely high-pitched.

MEXICAN SMILISCA (*Smilisca baudini*). Varies in color and pattern. Usually has large and irregular dark marks above. Sometimes uniformly grayish except for black stripe from tip of snout through nostril and eye; stripe may reach tympanum and shoulder. No other species has such a mark, especially at tip of snout. Male has paired vocal sacs. Mating call a stuttered hacking of 5–12 notes over 2–3 seconds, followed by a chuckle or two.

BURROWING TREEFROG (*Pternohyla fodiens*). Usually stays underground; is seen only after rains near desert pools. Light brown above, with large dark brown spots, ridge of skin just behind head, small toe pads. Underside is white. Male has paired vocal sacs, dark throat. Mating call a deep resonant squawk lasting 0.2–0.5 second and repeated 2–3 times a second.

NORTHERN CRICKET FROG (*Acris crepitans*). Small and warty, with dark triangle between eyes and no pads on toes. Color of this species quite varied. When hind leg is stretched out, dark stripe with ragged edges is seen on rear of thigh. First hind toe is completely webbed, 4th toe webbed at least to next-to-last phalanx. When hind leg is pressed forward, heel usually does not reach the snout. Male has single vocal sac. Mating call a rapid clicking. Two subspecies: (1) *A. c. crepitans*—wartier and bulkier, with clearer thigh stripe, than (2) *A. c. blanchardi*.

SOUTHERN CRICKET FROG (*Acris gryllus*). Resembles Northern Cricket but stripe or stripes on rear of thigh are sharp-edged. Also, 1st hind toe is completely webbed, usually the 3 terminal phalanges on 4th toe are not webbed, and the hind leg is longer than in Northern Cricket—when hind leg is pressed forward, heel extends beyond snout. Mating call of the Southern Cricket is a rapidly repeated metallic click. Three subspecies: (1) *A. g. gryllus*—single dark thigh stripe; (2) *A. g. dorsalis*—2 dark thigh stripes; (3) *A. g. paludicola*–1 dark thigh stripe, poorly defined; only last joint of 4th toe free of web.

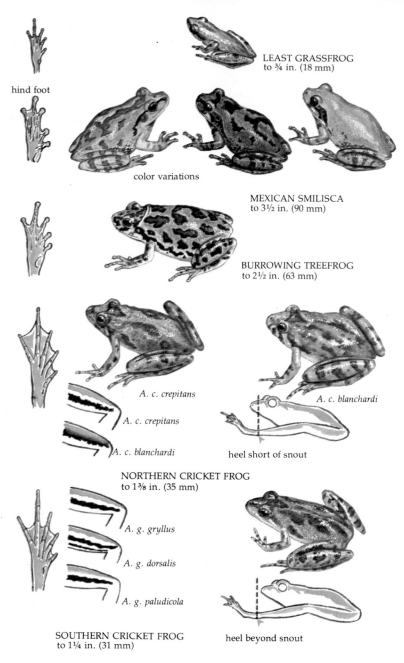

hind foot

LEAST GRASSFROG
to ¾ in. (18 mm)

color variations

MEXICAN SMILISCA
to 3½ in. (90 mm)

BURROWING TREEFROG
to 2½ in. (63 mm)

A. c. crepitans

A. c. crepitans

A. c. blanchardi

A. c. blanchardi

heel short of snout

NORTHERN CRICKET FROG
to 1⅜ in. (35 mm)

A. g. gryllus

A. g. dorsalis

A. g. paludicola

SOUTHERN CRICKET FROG
to 1¼ in. (31 mm)

heel beyond snout

49

CHORUS FROGS—genus *Pseudacris*

In eastern and central North America, these are the first frogs to appear in spring. They may chorus for as long as two months but after the breeding season are never heard—and rarely seen. Chorus frogs are ground dwellers. They have very small or no toe pads, climb only low plants. Tolerant to cold, they live as high as 11,000 feet in the Rocky Mountains and range as far north as the Arctic Circle in Canada. In all members, the feet are nearly webless.

As far as known, the genus is limited to North America. Mating calls of Strecker's and Ornate chorus frogs are a series of strident *cheeps*, 65–80 per minute, of sharply metallic quality. All other species produce trills similar to the sound made by pulling a thumb over the teeth of a comb from long teeth to short.

KEY TO CHORUS FROGS

1. Head wider than long .... *see* **2**
   Head as long as wide or longer ....
   ....*see* **4**
2. Tips of digits distinctly enlarged and padlike ....**Mountain,** p. 52
   Tips not enlarged .... *see* **3**
3. Dark spot on lip below eye ....
   .... **Strecker's,** below
   No dark spot on lip below eye .....
   .... **Ornate,** p. 52
4. 5 stripes, middle 3 distinctly lighter or faint; chest dark-spotted .... **Brimley's,** p. 52
   No stripes or all about equally dark; no spots on chest .....*see* **5**
5. Upper lip not or only faintly dark-edged; black-edged greenish spots or stripes ....
   ....**Spotted,** below
   Upper lip distinctly dark-edged; spots or stripes never green .....
   ....*see* **6**
6. Narrow white stripe on upper lip with narrow dark border beneath or broken by mottling; legs prominently light-barred ..
   ....**Southern,** p. 52
   Wide white stripe on upper lip with very narrow dark border beneath; legs not prominently barred .... **Northern,** p. 52

SPOTTED CHORUS FROG (*Pseudacris clarki*). This species is decorated with various patterns of greenish, black-edged spots (or rarely, stripes) and a similarly colored triangle between eyes. Upper lip may or may not have a faint dark edge. Has a large tympanum that nearly touches corner of mouth. Body is slender, head narrow.

STRECKER'S CHORUS FROG (*Pseudacris streckeri*). Usually gray to green or brown above, but sometimes nearly black. Irregular broken black stripe runs through the eye to shoulder. Irregular black spots mark sides. Dark spot below each eye. Body is stout, head broad. Two subspecies: (1) *P. s. streckeri*—side spots bold and contrasting, groin yellow to orange; (2) *P. s. illinoiensis*—side spots not contrasting, groin whitish.

IDENTIFYING CHORUS FROGS

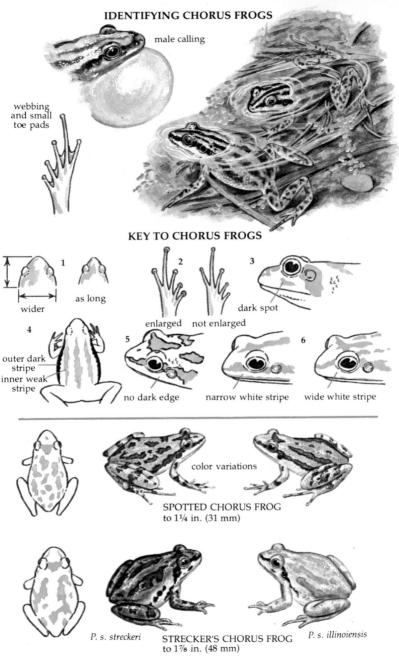

male calling

webbing and small toe pads

KEY TO CHORUS FROGS

1 wider / as long

2 enlarged / not enlarged

3 dark spot

4 outer dark stripe / inner weak stripe

5 no dark edge

narrow white stripe

6 wide white stripe

color variations

SPOTTED CHORUS FROG
to 1¼ in. (31 mm)

P. s. streckeri

STRECKER'S CHORUS FROG
to 1⅞ in. (48 mm)

P. s. illinoiensis

51

MOUNTAIN CHORUS FROG (*Pseudacris brachyphona*). Distinguishing this species are two dark stripes down the back that curve toward one another and sometimes fuse in the middle. The stripes are occasionally broken into rows of spots. Almost always a dark triangle is visible between the eyes. Body slender, head broad.

NORTHERN CHORUS FROG (*Pseudacris triseriata*). Has broad pale line on upper lip with well-defined dark border below; 3 stripes or rows of spots down back; poorly defined bars on hind legs, pale areas about as wide as the dark. Tympanum smaller than in Spotted Chorus (p. 50) and farther from corner of mouth. Body slender, head narrow. Three subspecies: (1) *P. t. triseriata*—stripes, shank one-third to one-half body length; (2) *P. t. feriarum*—stripes often thin, broken, or absent, shank one-half body length; (3) *P. t. maculata*—stripes or rows of spots, shank one-third body length. Some experts recognize (4) *P. t. kalmi*, Staten Isl. to Cape Charles, Va.; stouter, brighter stripes than (1).

BRIMLEY'S CHORUS FROG (*Pseudacris brimleyi*). This creature has 3 variable, sometimes indiscernible stripes running down its back. Also an always prominent, unbroken stripe along each side, extending from snout through eye to groin. No dark triangle is discernible between the eyes. Dark spots on chest. Body slender, head narrow.

SOUTHERN CHORUS FROG (*Pseudacris nigrita*). Generally very dark with rows of blackish spots or stripes down back. Narrow but conspicuous pale band, sometimes broken, on upper lip; no dark triangle between eyes. Hind legs have prominent, narrow, pale crossbars, separated by broad dark crossbands. Body slender, head narrow. Two subspecies: (1) *P. n. nigrita*—lip line unbroken, rows of spots on back frequently fused into stripes; (2) *P. n. verrucosa*—lip line broken by black and hardly evident, spots on back seldom fused.

ORNATE CHORUS FROG (*Pseudacris ornata*). Pale-bordered black stripe runs through eye to shoulder; pale-bordered black rounded spots are apparent on sides and groin. Back may be reddish or green, silvery to very dark; spotting also varies greatly. Concealed areas in groin are yellow. Body stout, head broad.

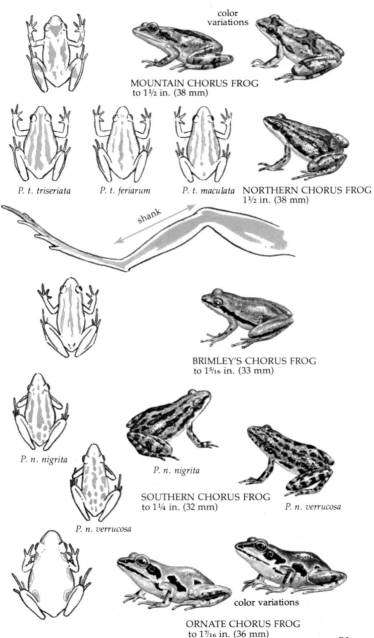

color variations

MOUNTAIN CHORUS FROG
to 1½ in. (38 mm)

P. t. triseriata   *P. t. feriarum*   *P. t. maculata*   **NORTHERN CHORUS FROG**
1½ in. (38 mm)

shank

BRIMLEY'S CHORUS FROG
to 1⁵/₁₆ in. (33 mm)

P. n. nigrita

P. n. nigrita

P. n. verrucosa

SOUTHERN CHORUS FROG
to 1¼ in. (32 mm)

P. n. verrucosa

color variations

ORNATE CHORUS FROG
to 1⁷/₁₆ in. (36 mm)

TRUE TREEFROGS—genus *Hyla*

All true treefrogs have an enlarged pad at the tip of each toe and are efficient climbers. The male's vocal sac is at mid-throat.

PACIFIC TREEFROG (*Hyla regilla*). Commonly green but often brown, tan, gray, or black, with or without dark streaks and spots between eyes. Black band extends through eye but never beyond shoulder. Small toe pads; very short webs on hind feet, no webs on front. Mating call a clear double-syllabled note repeated once a second. The frog call most often heard in movies.

CALIFORNIA TREEFROG (*Hyla cadaverina*). Grayish, often with rounded, diffuse-edged dark spots on back. Distinguished by large toe pads, half the size of tympanum; also by warty or rough skin. Mating call a succession of quick quacks; may be doubled-syllabled.

CANYON TREEFROG (*Hyla arenicolor*). Much like California but brownish, with less webbing between toes and a weakly bilobed (rather than round) vocal sac. Inhabits rocky areas near water. Mating call a pronounced slow buzz or trill of 1–3 seconds.

IDENTIFYING TRUE TREEFROGS

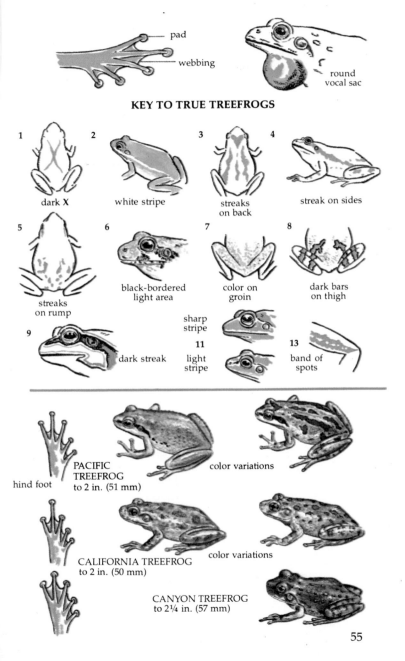

pad

webbing

round vocal sac

KEY TO TRUE TREEFROGS

1 dark **X**

2 white stripe

3 streaks on back

4 streak on sides

5 streaks on rump

6 black-bordered light area

7 color on groin

8 dark bars on thigh

9 dark streak

sharp stripe

11 light stripe

13 band of spots

hind foot

PACIFIC TREEFROG
to 2 in. (51 mm)

color variations

CALIFORNIA TREEFROG
to 2 in. (50 mm)

color variations

CANYON TREEFROG
to 2¼ in. (57 mm)

55

MOUNTAIN TREEFROG (*Hyla eximia*). Always greenish, dark or light. Dark band through eyes extends to groin. Toe pads small, one-half to three-fifths the size of tympanum. Webbing short between hind toes, slight between front. Lives in evergreen forests on ground or in trees. Mating call a rough clink like metal striking metal, repeated 1–3 times a second. U.S. subspecies: *H. e. wrightorum*.

GREATER GRAY TREEFROG (*Hyla versicolor*). This is the most widely distributed N.A. treefrog. Varies from green to gray, dark or light. Often bears large irregular marks, quite dark, on back. Concealed surfaces of legs are orange-tinted and dark-mottled. Two pads are large, some nearly tympanum-size; toe webs are extensive. Skin conspicuously warty. Despite extensive range, the species is limited to woody areas. On damp summer nights scattered males call repeatedly in a slow trill that lasts more than a second.

LESSER GRAY TREEFROG (*Hyla chrysocelis*). Much like Greater Gray, but lacks dark marks on rear of thigh and has fast trilling call that lasts less than 0.8 second. The range of this species is incompletely known and largely conjectural, as indicated on the map at left.

PEEPER TREEFROG (*Hyla crucifer*). Color of this species is always brownish, never greenish; pattern varies but almost always has X-shaped mark on back. Skin is smooth and toe pads rather small. Peepers breed in temporary pools in wooded regions. Mating call a whistle-like tone, clear and shrill, lasting 0.3 second and emitted once a second. Two subspecies: (1) *H. c. crucifer*—belly unmarked; (2) *H. c. bartramiana*—belly dark-spotted.

BIRD-VOICED TREEFROG (*Hyla avivoca*). Much like the Greater Gray but green, pale yellow, or white on concealed surfaces of legs. Also, somewhat smaller than the Greater Gray and has smoother skin; eyes somewhat larger proportionately. Mating call a resonant twittering of some 20 high-pitched notes a second. Two subspecies: (1) *H. a. avivoca*—to 1⅞ in. (49 mm), tympanum diameter averages 49 percent of eye diameter, concealed leg surfaces distinctly greenish; (2) *H. a. ogechiensis*—to 2¹/₁₆ in. (53 mm), tympanum diameter averages 53 percent of eye diameter; concealed leg surfaces are whitish.

hind foot

MOUNTAIN TREEFROG
to 2¼ in. (57 mm)

color variations

thigh
markings

GREATER GRAY TREEFROG
to 2⅜ in. (60 mm)

LESSER GRAY TREEFROG
to 1⅞ in. (48 mm)

H. c. crucifer   *H. c. bartramiana*

PEEPER TREEFROG
to 1⅜ in. (35 mm)

BIRD-VOICED TREEFROG
to 2¹⁄₁₆ (53 mm)

PINE BARRENS TREEFROG (*Hyla andersoni*). Green above, with white-bordered purplish stripe on sides and legs, orange on groin and rear of thigh. Toe pads are much smaller than tympanum. Skin smooth. Lives in swamps and bogs of pine barrens. Mating call a low honking repeated 20 or more times at intervals of 0.8 second. Rare and endangered.

GREEN TREEFROG (*Hyla cinerea*). Green, but gray when dormant. Almost always marked by a white stripe along each side and often by small yellow spots or flecks on back. Toe pads average half the size of tympanum. Found around still waters. Mating call resembles clink of cowbell, sounded once a second. Two subspecies: (1) *H. c. cinerea*—stripes usually extend to at least midbody; (2) *H. c. evittata*—stripes usually shorter.

PINE WOODS TREEFROG (*Hyla femoralis*). Color may be green without dark marks or brownish with irregular dark streaks and dark bar between eyes. Rear of thigh is dark with light spots. Toe pads are small, hind toe webs short. Skin smooth. Mating call a persistent vibratory clacking, 3–7 notes a second.

SQUIRREL TREEFROG (*Hyla squirella*). Color and pattern varied. May be green to brownish, with or without scattered dark marks. No markings on rear of thigh. Toe pads well developed. No webs on front toes; half webs on rear toes. Mating call a rough note sounded 15–20 times in 10 seconds; may resemble chattering squirrel.

CUBAN TREEFROG (*Osteopilus septentrionalis*). Largest N.A. treefrog north of Mexico. Back uniformly greenish to brownish or irregularly mottled. Skin fused to skull, giving head a striking appearance. Front toes slightly webbed, rear toes two-thirds webbed. Front toe pads as large as tympanum. Paired vocal sacs. Mating call a grating snore.

BARKING TREEFROG (*Hyla gratiosa*). Color varies from green to brownish above, usually with rounded spots often dim or absent in darker or lighter frogs. Some yellow on forelegs and throat. Body stout, skin granular, secretions musky. Toe pads about two-thirds size of tympanum; front toes partly webbed, hind toes fully webbed. Mating call a hollow bark every 1—*2 seconds*.

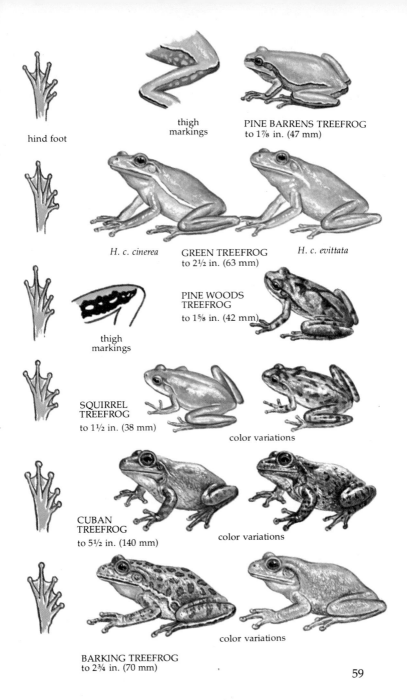

hind foot

thigh markings

PINE BARRENS TREEFROG
to 1⅞ in. (47 mm)

H. c. cinerea GREEN TREEFROG
to 2½ in. (63 mm) *H. c. evittata*

PINE WOODS TREEFROG
to 1⅝ in. (42 mm)

thigh markings

SQUIRREL TREEFROG
to 1½ in. (38 mm)

color variations

CUBAN TREEFROG
to 5½ in. (140 mm)

color variations

color variations

BARKING TREEFROG
to 2¾ in. (70 mm)

59

TRUE FROGS—family Ranidae

All of the 20 species of true frogs now recognized (certainly 1–3 yet to come) in North America north of Mexico belong to the genus *Rana*. Their life history is the typical one of most frogs and toads (p. 20).

KEY TO TRUE FROGS

1. Tympanum at least as large as eye; ridges never continuous for full length of body ...... *see* **2**
   Tympanum smaller than eye; ridges present and continuous or not .... *see* **7**
2. Alternating light and dark bands on concealed part of thigh .... *see* **3**
   No alternating bands .... *see* **5**
3. Some evidence of light stripes above; 2 segments of longest hind toe web-free ....**Carpenter,** p. 64
   No evidence of light stripes; no more than 1 segment of longest hind toe web-free .... *see* **4**
4. Hind-toe webs indented; 4th toe longer than others by at least last joint ....**Bullfrog,** p. 66
   Hind-toe webs not indented; 4th toe less than 1 joint longer than others ....**Pig,** p. 66
5. Tiny white spots on lips ....**River,** p. 64
   No white spots on lips .... *see* **6**
6. Ridges on sides of back distinct but not reaching groin ....**Green,** p. 66
   Ridges usually indistinct or absent ....**Mink,** p. 68
7. Dark mask through eye to tympanum, bordered below by white line .... *see* **8**
   No dark mask or light line ...*see* **11**
8. Reddish or yellowish suffusion on underside or on concealed surfaces of limbs; dark spots on back .... *see* **9**
   No reddish or yellowish coloring as above; no dark spots on back ....**Wood,** p. 64
9. Light stripe on upper lip to shoulder; eyes turned slightly upward; groin unmottled ....**Spotted,** p. 62
   Light stripe to tympanum; eyes not upturned; groin mottled .... *see* **10**

10. Many large, fuzzy-edged black spots ....**Red-legged,** p. 62
    Fewer black spots, distinctly outlined ....**Cascades,** p. 62
11. Square or somewhat rectangular spots in 2 rows on back and 2 rows on sides ....**Pickerel,** p. 68
    No such pattern .... *see* **12**
12. Tips on digits swollen as small discs; no light line on upper lip; no light borders on back spots .. ..**Tarahumara,** p. 64
    Tips on digits not enlarged; light line on upper lip or not; back spot light-bordered or not .... *see* **13**
13. No light line on upper lip, found E United States............. ....**Gopher,** p. 66
    Light line on upper lip of both lips, found W United States .... *see* **14**
14. Digits dark-tipped; dark spots on back never sharply outlined .... **Mountain Yellow-legged,** p. 62
    Digits not dark-tipped; dark spots sharply outlined or not ...*see* **15**
15. Ridges on back conspicuous; spots usually sharply outlined and light-bordered .... *see* **16**
    Ridges on back absent, irregular, or indistinct; spots never sharply outlined or light bordered ....**Foothill Yellow-legged,** p. 62
16. Throat and chest uniformly white ....**Northern, Southern,** or **Plains Leopard,** p. 68
    Throat and chest lightly dusted with dots in bright light, becoming dusky or mottled in darkness .... **Dusky Leopard,** p. 68

KEY TO TRUE FROGS

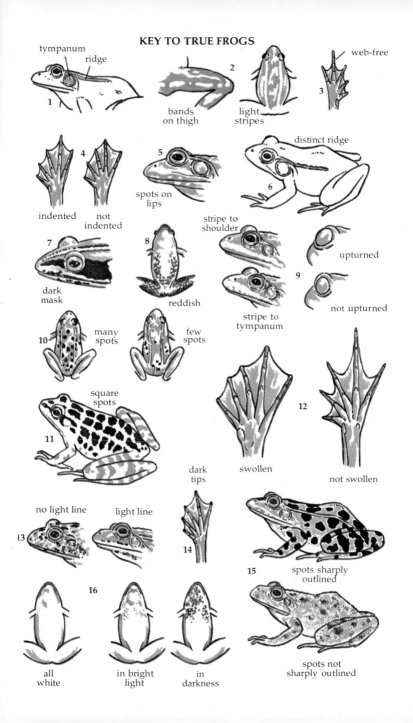

tympanum
ridge
1

bands on thigh
2
light stripes

web-free
3

4
indented   not indented

5
spots on lips

distinct ridge
6

7
dark mask

8
reddish

stripe to shoulder

upturned
9
not upturned

stripe to tympanum

10
many spots   few spots

square spots
11

12
swollen   not swollen

no light line   light line
13

dark tips
14

15
spots sharply outlined

16
all white   in bright light   in darkness

spots not sharply outlined

SPOTTED FROG (*Rana pretiosa*). Brownish above, marked by poorly defined or incomplete dark rings in a random pattern. Dark eye mask, sometimes faint, has pale border below. Usually well-developed but sometimes indistinct ridges on back. Eyes not fully covered by lids when viewed from above. Skin finely roughened. Undersides white in young, matures to red or yellow. Dark hues usually mottle the throat, sometimes entire frog. No mating call.

CASCADES FROG (*Rana cascadae*). Circular black markings on yellowish brown back and legs. Has dark mask bordered by pale line below. Well-developed ridges on back. Usually the rear undersurfaces and adjacent side areas are yellowish. Mating call a raspy baritone grunting, 4–5 notes a second.

RED-LEGGED FROG (*Rana aurora*). Gray above, may be red-tinged; thickish dark rings are interspersed with miniscule dark spots at reticulations. Dark mask through eyes is bordered below by pale line. Well-developed ridges along back. Groin darkly speckled, flecked with yellowish and reddish marks. Rear undersurface suffused with red or, in young, yellow. Strongly irritant skin secretions. Mating call an almost inaudible grumble or stammer ending with a slurred grunt; duration about 3 seconds. Two subspecies: (1) *R. a. aurora*—back spots smaller, lack pale centers; (2) *R. a. draytoni*—back spots larger, have pale centers.

FOOTHILL YELLOW-LEGGED FROG (*Rana boylei*). Gray to greenish, brownish, or reddish above, usually with thickly scattered dark spots. A paler triangle usually marks snout, triangle's baseline running from eyelid to eyelid. Yellow (never red) suffuses belly and hind legs. May have dark spots on throat and chest. Tympanum grainy. Always found close to water. Mating call a series of rather high-pitched grating notes of 1 second or less—resembles the clucking of domestic fowl.

MOUNTAIN YELLOW-LEGGED FROG (*Rana muscosa*). Much like Foothill but lip has prominent stripe. Also, usually lacks Foothill's pale triangle on head. Yellow on underside of hind legs often extends over abdomen to forelegs. Tips of digits are usually dark. Secretions have a garliclike odor. No mating call.

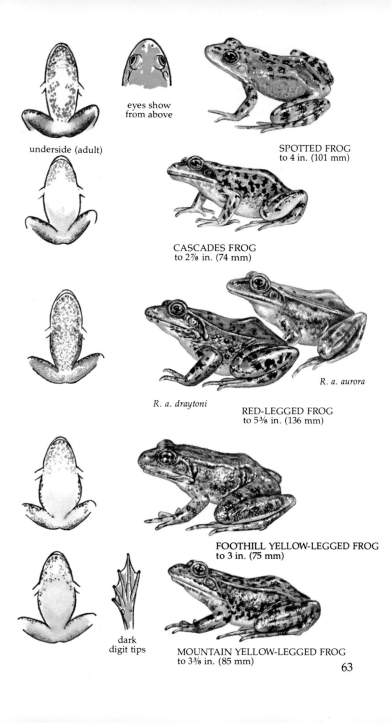

eyes show
from above

underside (adult)

SPOTTED FROG
to 4 in. (101 mm)

CASCADES FROG
to 2⅞ in. (74 mm)

R. a. draytoni

R. a. aurora

RED-LEGGED FROG
to 5⅜ in. (136 mm)

FOOTHILL YELLOW-LEGGED FROG
to 3 in. (75 mm)

dark
digit tips

MOUNTAIN YELLOW-LEGGED FROG
to 3⅜ in. (85 mm)

63

TARAHUMARA FROG (*Rana tarahumarae*). Only true frog in N.A. with small discs instead of sharp points at tip of toes. Found on wooded slopes of Pajarito Mts., S Arizona, within a few feet of water. Rear of thigh has large dark area marked by gray spots and streaks. Underside is immaculate white except for dark-clouded throat. Tympanum, sometimes indistinct, is two-fifths to one-half eye size; skin somewhat granular. No ridges along back, no mask, no pale line on side of head. No mating call.

WOOD FROG (*Rana sylvatica*). Distinguishable by dark facial mask bordered below by conspicuous pale line along jaw and tympanum. Otherwise varies greatly in color and pattern—ranging from immaculate light-to-reddish brown above and white below to dark with faint stripes above and rather profusely dark-flecked throat, chest, and anterior abdomen. Back and sides occasionally show vague dark spots. Ridges along back well developed; toes about half-webbed. Often Wood Frog individuals are found great distances from water, near which they do not linger even during the breeding season. Mating call a toneless, raspy quack. Four subspecies: (1) *R. s. sylvatica*—color usually uniform, body 53–62 percent as long as hind leg; (2) *R. s. cantabrigensis*—usually striped, body 62–75 percent as long as hind leg; (3) *R. s. latiremis*, usually striped, body three-fourths or more hind-leg length; (4) *R. s. maslini*—like (2) but call is slightly lower in pitch.

CARPENTER FROG (*Rana virgatipes*). Recognizable by 4 yellowish stripes and absence of ridges above. Has light line along lip and scattered indistinct dark spots on back. Two joints of the longest hind toe are free of web. Often found in sphagnum bogs. Males have lateral vocal sacs. Name refers to mating call, a double plunk resembling sound of a hammer striking nails.

RIVER FROG (*Rana heckscheri*). Color is greenish black above, heavily dark-mottled below. Lacks ridges along back. Fine pale dots mark jaw and lip areas. Rear of thigh mottled, not banded. Hind foot and eardrum much like Bullfrog's (p. 66); but skin rough, unlike Bullfrog's. Found in swamps near rivers, lakes. Mating call a low-pitched growl or snort.

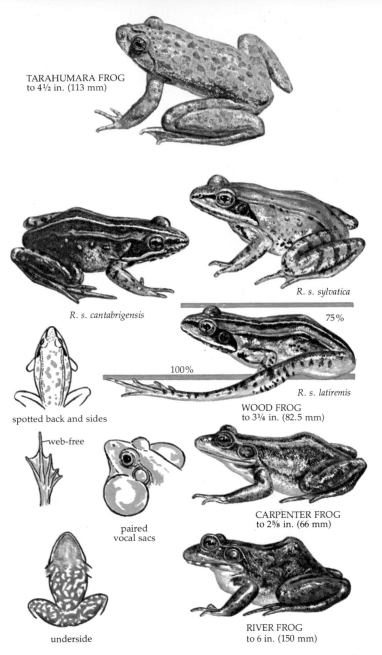

TARAHUMARA FROG
to 4½ in. (113 mm)

R. s. sylvatica

R. s. cantabrigensis

75%

100%

R. s. latiremis

spotted back and sides

web-free

paired
vocal sacs

underside

WOOD FROG
to 3¼ in. (82.5 mm)

CARPENTER FROG
to 2⅝ in. (66 mm)

RIVER FROG
to 6 in. (150 mm)

PIG FROG (*Rana grylio*). Olive to brown back sprinkled with darker flecks; belly pale but laced with dusky markings. No ridges along back. In contrast to Bullfrog, webs on hind feet reach tips of toes, and longest toe is only slightly longer than others. Mating call sounds like a hog grunting, hence the name.

BULLFROG (*Rana catesbyiana*). The largest N.A. frog. Green to olive or brown above, grading to green toward head, with a few indistinct markings on back. Usually has conspicuous bands on hind legs. Underside pale, may have dusky markings. Throat of male is suffused with yellow. Ridges extend from eye around tympanum but not along back. Longest toe on each hind foot extends slightly beyond webbing. Tympanum larger in males. Mating call a deep, reverberating *br-wum*, roarlike. Startled Bullfrogs may emit a catlike *meow* as they leap into water.

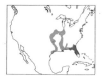

GREEN FROG (*Rana clamitans*). Color is green to brown above, immaculately white or darkly flecked or reticulated below. Distinct ridges extend from head two-thirds the length of body. Tympanum, as among Bullfrogs, is a little larger in males. Mating call of the Green is a deep *tung* like the sound of the lowest string of a banjo. Two subspecies: (1) *R. c. clamitans*—smaller, immaculate brownish above, reticulated below; (2) *R. c. melanota*— green to brown with dark spots above, mostly white below, legs and throat mottled.

GOPHER FROG (*Rana areolata*). Distinguished by wide head, chunky body, many oval or rounded spots on back and sides, well-developed ridges on back. Frequents holes made by gopher tortoises, crayfish, etc. Males have lateral vocal sacs. Mating call a deep roaring snore. Five subspecies: (1) *R. a. areolata*—pale-bordered dark spots, belly white, skin nearly smooth; (2) *R. a. circulosa*—same as (1) but larger and wartier, head shorter and broader, ridges more prominent; (3) *R. a. capito*—spots not pale-bordered, white belly heavily dark-flecked, warty, smaller; (4) *R. a. sevosa*—much like (3) but back almost as dark as spots, belly sometimes less heavily dark-flecked; (5) *R. a. aesopus*—color very light, dark spots not pale-bordered, chin and throat spotted, skin nearly smooth.

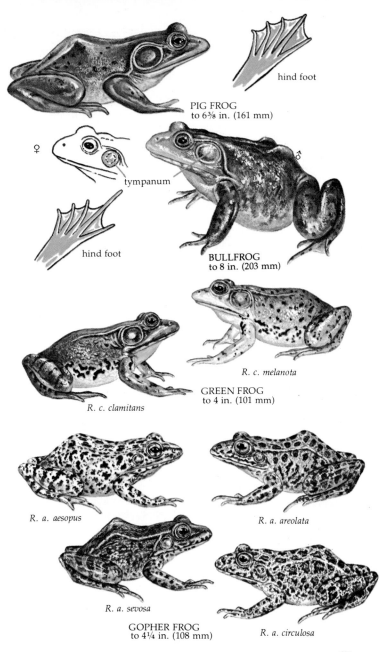

hind foot

PIG FROG
to 6⅜ in. (161 mm)

♀

tympanum

hind foot

♂

BULLFROG
to 8 in. (203 mm)

R. c. melanota

R. c. clamitans

GREEN FROG
to 4 in. (101 mm)

R. a. aesopus

R. a. areolata

R. a. sevosa

GOPHER FROG
to 4¼ in. (108 mm)

R. a. circulosa

NORTHERN LEOPARD FROG (*Rana pipiens*). Green or brown with sharply defined light-bordered dark spots; sometimes only a dark peppering or mottling on lighter background. Conspicuous back ridges, slender body, sharp nose, moderate webbing, pale stripe on upper lip. Mating call a gruff chuckling lasting ⅔-5 seconds, varied with resonant moans and grunts. With following four species, once thought to be one species over all of N.A. Taxonomy still not adequately understood.

SOUTHERN LEOPARD FROG (*Rana sphenocephala*). Spots average smaller than eye; not light-bordered. Snout usually lacks spot. Breeding males show external vocal sacs. Ridges like Northern Leopard's; mating call shorter, vibrations slower.

PLAINS LEOPARD FROG (*Rana blairi*). Resembles Northern, but back ridges broken near hind legs. Mating call 2–3 henlike clucks a second.

VEGAS VALLEY LEOPARD FROG (*Rana onca*). Spots weaker, smaller, and less well defined than spots of other *Rana* species. External vocal sac. Mating call uncertain. Now thought to be extinct. [No range map.]

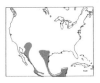

DUSKY LEOPARD FROG (*Rana berlandieri*). Paler version of Plains. Back ridges broken. In bright light, throat and chest show faint dots imparting a dusky or mottled appearance. Subspecies poorly known but two seem valid in U.S.: (1) *R. b. berlandieri*—groin greenish or whitish; (2) *R. b.* unnamed—groin yellow-orange.

PICKEREL FROG (*Rana palustris*). Known by dark rectangular markings on back and sides; limbs may be yellow-orange below. Ridges conspicuous; skin exudes acrid liquid, poisonous to some creatures. Mating call a gruff snore lasting a second or so.

MINK FROG (*Rana septentrionalis*). Tan to green above, with scattered to densely packed dark patches. Green sometimes pronounced on lower jaw and chest. Thigh darkly marked or reticulated. Back ridges rarely well developed, may be absent. When disturbed, gives off garliclike odor resembling mink's. Toe webbing nearly full. Mating call a swift succession of low metallic-sounding clucks.

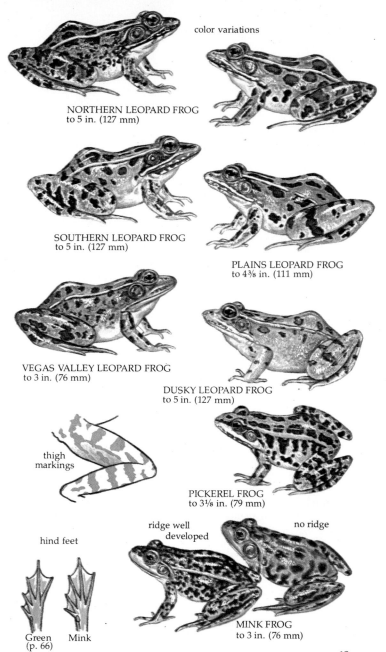

color variations

NORTHERN LEOPARD FROG
to 5 in. (127 mm)

SOUTHERN LEOPARD FROG
to 5 in. (127 mm)

PLAINS LEOPARD FROG
to 4⅜ in. (111 mm)

VEGAS VALLEY LEOPARD FROG
to 3 in. (76 mm)

DUSKY LEOPARD FROG
to 5 in. (127 mm)

thigh
markings

PICKEREL FROG
to 3⅛ in. (79 mm)

hind feet

Green
(p. 66)   Mink

ridge well
developed

no ridge

MINK FROG
to 3 in. (76 mm)

69

SALAMANDERS—order Caudata

Of the eight families, 54 genera, and 341 species of salamanders now known worldwide, 27 genera and 112 species inhabit North America north of Mexico. Unlike frogs and toads, salamanders possess a slender body, a long tail, and usually four legs of about equal length. In a few salamander species, the sirens (p. 78), hind legs are missing. Most salamanders have true teeth in both jaws, whereas frogs and toads lack lower teeth. Although salamanders are often confused with lizards, the two can easily be distinguished. Lizards possess scales, claws, and ear openings; salamanders do not.

All North American salamanders lay eggs. Except in the Hellbender (p. 76) and among the sirens (p. 78), the eggs of all North American salamanders are fertilized internally. After performing a stereotyped courtship ritual that differs only in detail from one group to another, the male deposits jellylike capsules of sperm called spermatophores. The female picks them up with the lips of the cloaca, the chamber through which eggs and wastes pass to the outside. The sperm are usually stored near the cloacal opening, remaining there to fertilize the eggs as they are laid. In the Hellbender and the siren salamanders, the eggs are fertilized outside the body, the male releasing sperm over them after they have been laid in water by the female.

Males and females of most species look much alike except during the breeding season when the most conspicuous difference is a swollen gland around the male's vent. This gland produces the spermatophore, which carries the sperm packet at its tip. The cloacal walls bear papillae in males, as can be seen with a hand lens or microscope. The area around the vent is not swollen in females, and the cloacal walls are smooth or ridged.

Most salamanders lay their eggs in water, some on land in deep cavities. The young that hatch on land look much like small adults. But those that hatch in water breathe through gills and have skin hooding the eyes. These larvae differ from tadpoles of frogs and toads in several ways: the salamander larva develops legs early in life and has external gills on the neck; the head is distinct from the body and, seen from above, is broader than the body. After some months, the larvae of most salamanders transform into adults and leave the water. They lose their gills and grow eyelids. Some develop lungs; others "breathe" through their moist skin. Some aquatic larvae, like those of the mudpuppies and waterdogs (p. 74), are neotenic—that is, they retain their gills and remain in the water, where they become sexually mature.

Whether on land or in water, salamanders are inconspicuous. They spend much of the time hidden beneath stones or other objects. With few exceptions they make no sounds.

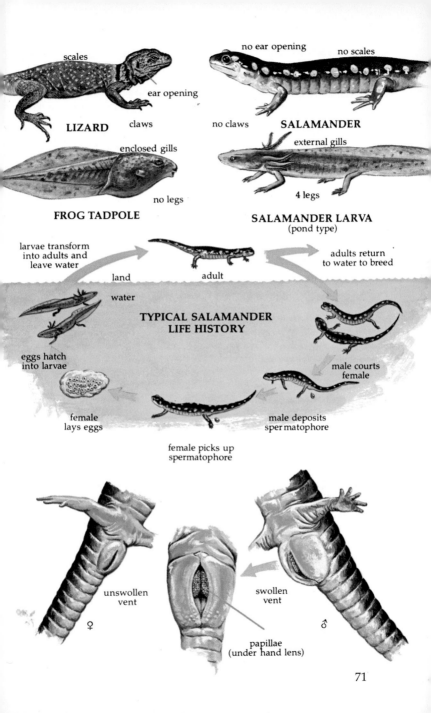

scales

ear opening

LIZARD

claws

no ear opening

no scales

no claws

SALAMANDER

external gills

4 legs

enclosed gills

no legs

FROG TADPOLE

SALAMANDER LARVA
(pond type)

larvae transform
into adults and
leave water

land

adult

water

**TYPICAL SALAMANDER
LIFE HISTORY**

eggs hatch
into larvae

female
lays eggs

adults return
to water to breed

male courts
female

male deposits
spermatophore

female picks up
spermatophore

unswollen
vent

♀

swollen
vent

♂

papillae
(under hand lens)

71

IDENTIFICATION. Important characteristics, aside from color and pattern, include tongue, teeth, costal grooves, and gill slits. A hand lens or microscope is needed to examine tongue and teeth. To open the mouth, gently insert a thin strip of stiff plastic and carefully nudge apart the jaws. Although salamander teeth occupy the margins of both jaws, the teeth significant for identification are located as a rule in the roof of the mouth and lie between the rows of marginal teeth.

Costal grooves are vertical grooves in the sides of the body between the front and the back limbs. These grooves correspond in position to the vertebrae and ribs. The presence or absence of grooves, and especially their number, are important aids to identification. To determine the identifying number, count all the grooves between the two limbs on one side only; if the distance from axilla (armpit) or groin to the nearest complete groove equals or exceeds half the distance between other grooves, count an extra groove. Instead of grooves, some experts count costal folds—the spaces between grooves. One reason the number of costal grooves between appressed limbs so often helps identification is that it tells the relation of leg length to body length. To determine this, press the salamander's front leg back along the side of the body and the corresponding rear leg forward, then count the grooves between the tips of the toes. The fewer grooves visible, the longer the legs in relation to the body.

Gill slits consist of one to four vertical openings at the base of the gills in each side of the neck of the larvae. In most species the larvae lose both gill slits and gills in transforming to adults. In some species, however, adults retain gill slits along with gills. In very few, gills are lost but one or more gill slits remain.

KEY TO SALAMANDER FAMILIES

1. Long cylindrical eel-like body .....
   ....*see* **2**
   Not eel-like ....*see* **3**
2. Diminutive rear limbs ....
   ....**amphiumas,** p. 76
   No rear limbs ....**sirens,** p. 78
3. Gills present ....**larval forms,** *see* **7**
   No gills ....**adult forms,** *see* **4**
4. (*not shown*) Gill slits present ....
   ....**giant salamanders,** p. 76
   No gill slits ....*see* **5**
5. Costal grooves present ....*see* **6**
   No costal grooves ...**newts,** p. 130
6. Nasolabial groove present ....
   .....**lungless salamanders,** p. 90
   No nasolabial groove ....
   ....**mole salamanders,** p. 80
7. 3 gill slits ....
   .....**lungless salamanders,** p. 90
   0, 2, or 4 gill slits ....*see* **8**

8. (*not shown*) 4 rear toes ....**mud-puppies** and **waterdogs,** p. 74
   5 rear toes ....*see* **9**
9. Palatal teeth in patches ....*see* **10**
   Palatal teeth absent or in rows .....
   ....*see* **11**
10. Maxillary teeth present ....
    ...**true mole salamanders,** p. 82
    No maxillary teeth ....
    ....**newts,** p. 130
11. Maxillary teeth present ....*see* **12**
    No maxillary teeth ....
    .....**lungless salamanders,** p. 90
12. Fin on tail only ....
    ...**true mole salamanders,** p. 82
    Fin extending onto body ....
    ....**giant salamanders,** p. 76

72

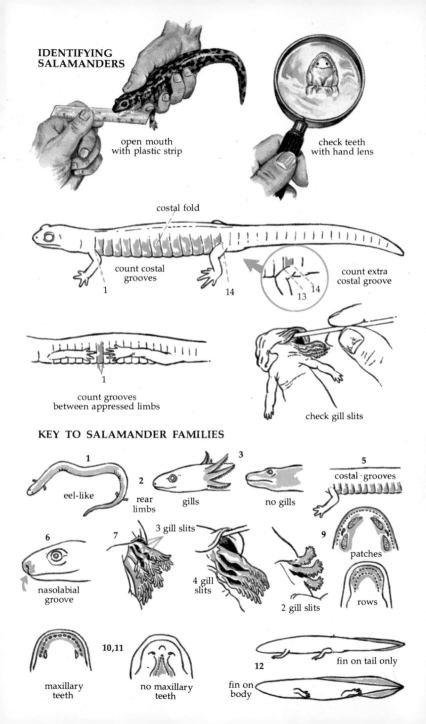

IDENTIFYING SALAMANDERS

open mouth with plastic strip

check teeth with hand lens

costal fold

count costal grooves

1   14

count extra costal groove

13   14

count grooves between appressed limbs

1

check gill slits

KEY TO SALAMANDER FAMILIES

1 eel-like

2 rear limbs

3 gills

no gills

5 costal grooves

6 nasolabial groove

7 3 gill slits

4 gill slits

2 gill slits

9 patches

rows

maxillary teeth

10,11 no maxillary teeth

12 fin on tail only

fin on body

MUDPUPPIES AND WATERDOGS—family Necturidae

The names of these salamanders derive from the mistaken belief that they bark like dogs—but they can only squeak. In the main they live in streams, lakes, and ditches. They wear feathery red gills throughout life. Four toes rather than the usual five characterize each rear foot; a short tail accounts for a third or less of body length. The female attaches 18–125 eggs singly to the undersides of submerged objects. The female of the Mudpuppy, the commonest species, guards eggs until they hatch—in 38 to 63 days, depending on temperature. Larvae, three-fourths of an inch long at hatching, mature in five years or less, depending on latitude. Experts disagree regarding classification, hence validity of the five species below is somewhat questionable.

KEY TO MUDPUPPIES AND WATERDOGS

1. Belly all colored, spotted ......*see* **2**
   Not as above ....*see* **4**
2. Back no darker than belly ....*see* **3**
   Darker ....***N. m. maculosus,*** below
3. Few large dark spots on back ......
   ....**Neuse River,** below
   Many small ....**Gulf Coast,** below

4. Dark spots clearly evident on back,
   belly, or both ....*see* **5**
   Not clear anywhere ....
   ....**Dwarf,** below
5. Most of belly uncolored and un-
   spotted ....**Alabama,** below
   Narrow midstrip of belly only......
   ....***N. m. louisianensis,*** below

MUDPUPPY (*Necturus maculosus*). Orange-brown to gray above; lighter below, with spots. Larva usually has light line on each side of back. Two subspecies: (1) *N. m. maculosus*—entire belly pigmented, spotted; (2) *N. m. louisianensis*—center strip of belly unpigmented, unspotted. Some authorities recognize a third subspecies, *N. m. stictus,* in NE Wisconsin and adjacent Michigan.

DWARF WATERDOG (*Necturus punctatus*). Brownish above, with scant or no spots; whitish and unspotted below. No subspecies.

ALABAMA WATERDOG (*Necturus alabamensis*). Brown above, with a few large dark spots. Mostly uncolored and unmarked below. Two subspecies: (1) *N. a. alabamensis*—darker above; (2) *N. a. lodingi*—lighter above.

NEUSE RIVER WATERDOG (*Necturus lewisi*). Back orange-brown, with well-defined dark spots. Smaller spots on pigmented belly.

GULF COAST WATERDOG (*Necturus beyeri*). Uniformly brown. Many dark spots above and below.

FAMILY CHARACTERISTICS OF MUDPUPPIES AND WATERDOGS

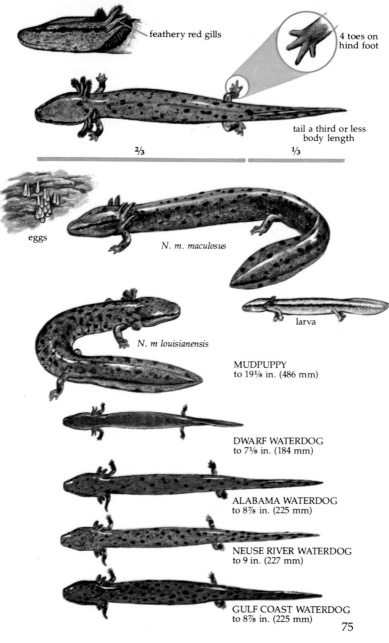

feathery red gills

4 toes on hind foot

tail a third or less body length

2/3

1/3

eggs

N. m. maculosus

N. m louisianensis

larva

MUDPUPPY
to 19⅛ in. (486 mm)

DWARF WATERDOG
to 7⅛ in. (184 mm)

ALABAMA WATERDOG
to 8⅞ in. (225 mm)

NEUSE RIVER WATERDOG
to 9 in. (227 mm)

GULF COAST WATERDOG
to 8⅞ in. (225 mm)

75

GIANT SALAMANDERS—family Cryptobranchidae

This family is represented in North America by one species, the Hellbender. (Two other species live in Asia. The Giant Salamander of Japan, the largest living salamander, reaches a length of 5½ feet.)

 **HELLBENDER** (*Cryptobranchus alleganiensis*). Ugly, frighteningly large—but harmless—nocturnal salamander found in streams and rivers, often under rocks. Broad flat head; a loose flap of skin on each side of the body, also folds or creases elsewhere. Brown or gray above, often with scattered dark spots; lighter below. Adults usually have a gill slit concealed on each side of the neck. Two subspecies: (1) *C. a. alleganiensis*—few dark spots on throat, small spots on back and tail; (2) *C. a. bishopi*—many prominent dark spots on throat, large dark patches on body and tail.

AMPHIUMAS—family Amphiumidae

These aquatic salamanders have an eel-like body with four tiny limbs. They live in muddy swamps, ditches, sloughs, ponds, and streams, feeding on small animals. They are nocturnal, commonly spending the day under objects at the water's edge. Amphiumas bite viciously. Females guard strings of eggs laid in nestlike depressions. The larvae do not transform completely; they lose their gills before reaching 3 inches in length but permanently retain one pair of gill slits. To tell the three species apart, simply count toes on any limb.

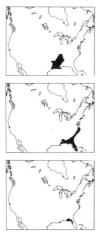 **THREE-TOED AMPHIUMA** (*Amphiuma tridactylum*). Rather uniform deep brown above, abruptly changing to pearly or smoke-gray below. Tail 18–28 percent of animal's length; 60–64 costal grooves. Foreleg when pressed forward overlaps gill slit; hind leg when pressed backward overlaps vent.

TWO-TOED AMPHIUMA (*Amphiuma means*). Deep brown to black above, grading into slate below. Costal grooves, 57–60. Tail and limb proportions are similar to those of Three-toed.

ONE-TOED AMPHIUMA (*Amphiuma pholeter*). Gray-brown above, somewhat lighter below. Tail about 23 percent of animal's length; some 65 costal grooves. Foreleg when pressed forward at best barely reaches gill slit; hind leg when pressed backward falls short of vent.

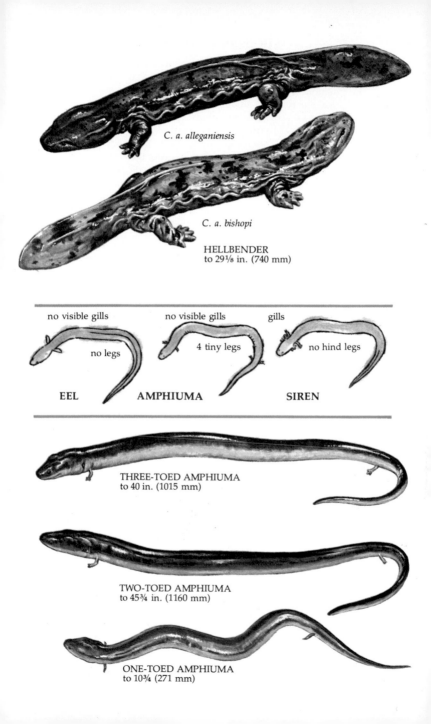

C. a. alleganiensis

C. a. bishopi

HELLBENDER
to 29⅛ in. (740 mm)

no visible gills

no legs

EEL

no visible gills

4 tiny legs

AMPHIUMA

gills

no hind legs

SIREN

THREE-TOED AMPHIUMA
to 40 in. (1015 mm)

TWO-TOED AMPHIUMA
to 45¾ in. (1160 mm)

ONE-TOED AMPHIUMA
to 10¾ (271 mm)

SIRENS—family Sirenidae

The sirens are among the most unusual of all salamanders. Their most distinctive feature, unique to the family, is the absence of hind limbs. The forelimbs are moderately well developed. All three species are cylindrical like eels and retain large gills. Fully aquatic, these creatures are found in shallow streams, ponds, and lakes in the South. They eat worms, crayfish, and other small aquatic animals.

Actual mating of sirens has never been observed. Their anatomy indicates that the male fertilizes the eggs after they have been laid, but the scattered eggs, laid singly or in small clumps on submerged plants, suggest internal fertilization. Sirens become sexually mature while still in a larval stage; they never transform from the larval to the adult form and cannot be induced to do so by any known drug. Two genera of the siren family live in North America north of Mexico: *Siren* (two species) and *Pseudobranchus*, the dwarf siren (one species).

LESSER SIREN (*Siren intermedia*). Sides and green-to-chocolate back are darkly spotted. Pointed tail accounts for about a third of animal's length. Has 4 toes, 3 gill slits, no stripes, and forelegs more than half the length of the head. Costal grooves, 31–38. Three subspecies: (1) *S. i. intermedia*—31–33 costal grooves; (2) *S. i. nettingi*—34–36 costal grooves; (3) *S. i. texana*—37–38 costal grooves.

GREATER SIREN (*Siren lacertina*). Distinguished by fine yellowish streaks on back and sides; many yellow dots scattered over belly; sometimes large black spots appear on sides and back. Rounded tail is slightly less than a third of animal's length. Has 4 toes, 3 gill slits, no stripes, and forelegs more than half the length of the head. Costal grooves, 36–39.

DWARF SIREN (*Pseudobranchus striatus*). Differs from other sirens in having a pale-striped body, 3 toes, 1 gill slit, forelegs less than half as long as the head, and 29–37 costal grooves. Five subspecies: (1) *P. s. striatus*—yellow stripe on each side is about half width of dark area on back; (2) *P. s. axanthus*—faint buff or grayish side stripes; (3) *P. s. belli*—beige or tan side stripes; (4) *P. s. lustricolus*—definite yellow striping down middle of back; (5) *P. s. spheniscus*—beige to yellow stripes much less than half the width of dark central band on back.

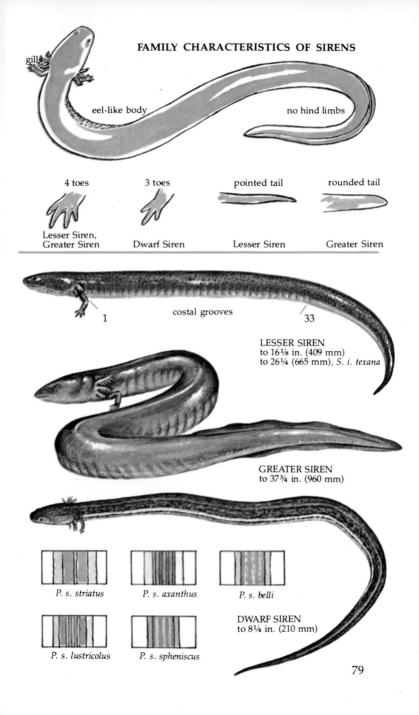

FAMILY CHARACTERISTICS OF SIRENS

gills

eel-like body

no hind limbs

4 toes
Lesser Siren,
Greater Siren

3 toes
Dwarf Siren

pointed tail
Lesser Siren

rounded tail
Greater Siren

1 costal grooves 33

LESSER SIREN
to 16⅛ in. (409 mm)
to 26¼ (665 mm), *S. i. texana*

GREATER SIREN
to 37¾ in. (960 mm)

P. s. striatus

P. s. axanthus

P. s. belli

P. s. lustricolus

P. s. spheniscus

DWARF SIREN
to 8¼ in. (210 mm)

79

MOLE SALAMANDERS—family Ambystomatidae

These salamanders commonly burrow in the ground, as their name suggests. They are set apart from other families by a combination of characteristics, including well-developed costal grooves (in all except Pacific Giant and Cope's Giant), four stout limbs, four toes on each front foot and five on each rear. Larvae have a tail fin that extends over the back at least halfway to the head. In early life the larvae of most species have well-developed balancers, poorly developed or absent in other families. Balancers may help the mole salamanders keep their gills out of the bottom muck of ponds. Three genera live in North America north of Mexico: *Dicamptodon* (two species), *Rhyacotriton* (one species), and *Ambystoma*, the true salamanders (14 or 15 species).

KEY TO ADULT MOLE SALAMANDERS

1. Eye width less than eye-to-snout distance ....*see* **2**
   Eye width equal to or more than eye-to-snout distance ....
   ....**Olympic,** below
2. (*not shown*) Indistinct costal grooves ....*see* **3**

   Distinct costal grooves ....
   ....**true mole salamanders,** p. 82
3. Head width less than one-fifth snout-to-vent length ....
   ....**Cope's Giant** below
   Head width more than one-fifth snout-to-vent length ....
   ....**Pacific Giant,** below

MOLE SALAMANDERS—genus *Dicamptodon*
and genus *Rhyacotriton*

PACIFIC GIANT SALAMANDER (*Dicamptodon ensatus*). Inhabits damp coastal forests. Large and heavy-bodied, indistinct costal grooves. Larvae hatch from large colorless eggs laid singly in underground springs, then swim to streams or lakes. They may or may not transform into adults; larvae can produce progeny.

COPE'S GIANT SALAMANDER (*Dicamptodon copei*). Similar to Pacific Giant, but smaller and with proportionately narrower head. Larvae distinguished by a netted pattern of dark brown on a yellowish tan background. No transformed adult has ever been found; apparently this salamander breeds while still in larval stage.

OLYMPIC SALAMANDER (*Rhyacotriton olympicus*). Lives in forests in or beside streams or springs. Has large eyes. Males have angular (not rounded) lobes around vent. Larvae all transform. Costal grooves, 14–15. Two subspecies: (1) *R. o. olympicus*—belly yellowish or orange with few or no dark spots; (2) *R. o. variegatus*—belly light green or yellow with many black spots.

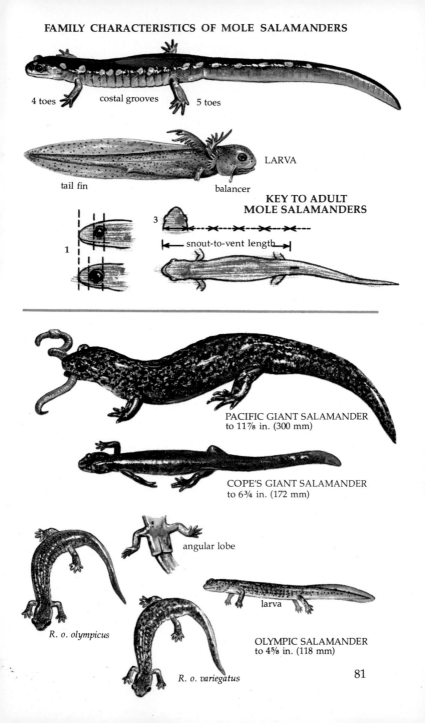

FAMILY CHARACTERISTICS OF MOLE SALAMANDERS

4 toes   costal grooves   5 toes

tail fin   balancer   LARVA

KEY TO ADULT MOLE SALAMANDERS

1

3

snout-to-vent length

PACIFIC GIANT SALAMANDER
to 1⅞ in. (300 mm)

COPE'S GIANT SALAMANDER
to 6¾ in. (172 mm)

angular lobe

larva

R. o. olympicus

R. o. variegatus

OLYMPIC SALAMANDER
to 4⅝ in. (118 mm)

81

TRUE MOLE SALAMANDERS—genus *Ambystoma*

True mole salamanders lay small colorless eggs in water. An exception is the Marbled Salamander (p. 84), which lays its eggs on land. Larvae of the Tiger, Talpid, and Northwestern salamanders (pp. 84, 86) may transform to land-dwelling adults or may remain in the larval form throughout their life span. Larvae of all other true mole species eventually lose their gills and transform.

These salamanders are often difficult to distinguish from members of the lungless family (p. 90) but can be recognized by the absence of a nasolabial groove running between the lip and the nostrils. The larvae can sometimes be identified by geographic location.

Two major subgenera of *Ambystoma* are *Linguaelapsus*, including Ringed, Small-mouth, Flatwoods, and Mabee's salamanders (pp. 84, 86), all with tongue grooves branching from a central front-to-rear groove, and (except Mabee's) several rows of jaw-margin teeth; and *Ambystoma* (all other species), with tongue grooves radiating from rear of tongue, one row of jaw-margin teeth.

KEY TO ADULT TRUE MOLE SALAMANDERS

1. Found W of 100th meridian ..*see* **2**
   Found E of 100th meridian ....*see* **4**
2. Light back stripe ....
   ....**Long-toed,** p. 86
   No light back stripe ....*see* **3**
3. Bold mottling ....**Tiger,** p. 84
   Light flecks or no markings at all
   ....**Northwestern,** p. 86
4. Light bars or spots across dark
   back ....*see* **5**
   Scattered or no fuzzy light marks
   on dark back ....*see* **6**
5. (*not shown*) Light underside ....
   ....**Ringed,** p. 84
   Dark underside ....**Marbled,** p. 84
6. 10–11 costal grooves; no sharply
   defined light or dark spots
   ....**Talpid,** p. 86
   Usually more than 11 costal
   grooves; sharply defined spots
   may be present ....*see* **7**
7. 1–2 tubercles on sole of foot ....
   ....*see* **8**
   No tubercles on sole of foot ....
   ....*see* **9**
8. Row of round light spots on each
   side of back; no light markings
   on sides ....**Spotted,** p. 84
   Light spots, if present, more numerous, some oval or extending onto sides ....**Tiger,** p. 84

9. (*not shown*) 13–15 costal grooves
   ....*see* **10**
   12 costal grooves ....*see* **12**
10. Light flecks usually form narrow
    vertical bands on sides ....
    ....**Flatwoods,** p. 86
    Light flecks scattered or absent ....
    ....*see* **11**
11. (*not shown*) 13 costal grooves ....
    ....**Mabee's,** p. 86
    14–15 costal grooves
    ....**Small-mouth,** p. 84
12. Nostrils narrow-set, less than ⁵/₃₂
    in. (4 mm) ....*see* **13**
    Nostrils wide-set, more than ⁵/₃₂
    in. (4 mm) ....*see* **14**
13. (*not shown*) Total length usually
    5¹/₈ in. (129 mm) or more; not
    male ....**Tremblay's,** p. 88
    Total length always less than 5¹/₈
    in. (129 mm); may be male ....
    ....**Blue-spotted,** p. 88
14. (*not shown*) Rarely more than ³/₁₆
    in. (4.6 mm); not male.............
    ....**Tremblay's,** p. 88
    Distance between nostrils ³/₁₆ in.
    (4.6 mm) or more; may be male
    ......**Jefferson's** or **Silvery,** p. 88

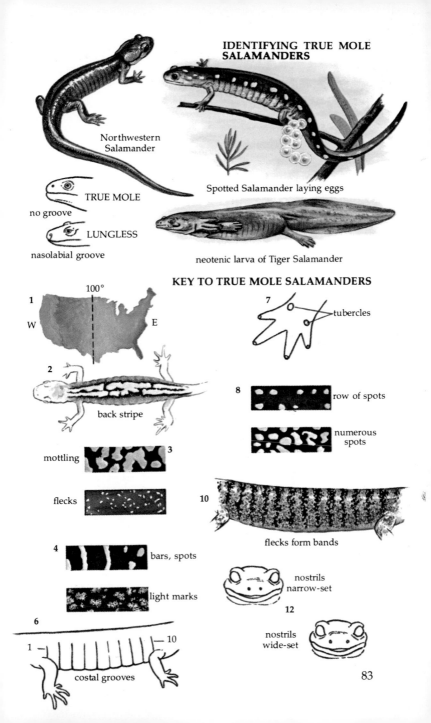

IDENTIFYING TRUE MOLE SALAMANDERS

Northwestern Salamander

Spotted Salamander laying eggs

TRUE MOLE
no groove

LUNGLESS
nasolabial groove

neotenic larva of Tiger Salamander

KEY TO TRUE MOLE SALAMANDERS

1 100°
W E

7 tubercles

2 back stripe

8 row of spots
numerous spots

mottling **3**
flecks

10 flecks form bands

4 bars, spots
light marks

nostrils narrow-set

6
1 — — 10
costal grooves

12 nostrils wide-set

83

TIGER SALAMANDER (*Ambystoma tigrinum*). World's largest terrestrial salamander. Frequents cellars, mammal burrows, other damp dark places. Commonly breeds in small ponds; larvae lack balancers. Some adults are spotted, some not. Soles of feet have 1 or 2 tubercles. Costal grooves, 11–14, usually 12 or 13. Subspecies: (1) *A. t. californiense*—dark gray with yellowish spots on sides; geographically isolated, now regarded by many authorities as a full species, the California Tiger; (2) *A. t. tigrinum*—profusely blotched with brown to yellow spots; (3) *A. t. mavortium*—yellowish bars or patches on sides; (4) *A. t. nebulosum*—all dark, or dark marks on gray to cream ground; (5) *A. t. melanostictum*—yellow mesh on dark ground; (6) *A. t. diaboli*—dark spots on olive; (7) *A. t. stebbinsi*—25–45 pale spots on back between forelegs and hind legs.

SPOTTED SALAMANDER (*Ambystoma maculatum*). Found under debris in deciduous forests near ponds or slow streams lacking fish. Black to dark brown above, usually with row of 12–22 yellow, cream, or orange eye-sized spots along each side of back from head to tail. Gray to nearly black below. Costal grooves, 11–13.

RINGED SALAMANDER (*Ambystoma annulatum*). Lives in damp hilly areas, open or forested. Brown to black above; "rings" are creamy to yellow crossbars or patches along back from head to tail; pattern variable. Dark interspaces much wider than pale bars, which merge on sides with lead-colored streak between limbs. Dusky gray below, speckled with white. Costal grooves, 15.

MARBLED SALAMANDER (*Ambystoma opacum*). Found under debris in damp woods near ponds or slow streams. Black above and below, with 4 to 7 transverse white to pewter bars sometimes fusing. Pattern poorly developed in newly transformed adults. Costal grooves, 11–12. Breeds in fall; lays eggs on land. Female tends eggs until rains flood hollow where laid.

SMALL-MOUTH SALAMANDER (*Ambystoma texanum*). Lives in forested, grassy, or farmed moist plains or lowlands, often in deserted crayfish holes. Head narrow, mouth small. Brown to black back, lighter belly; both usually with grayish flecks of varying shape, size, and intensity. Has 14–15 costal grooves.

A. t. californiense

A. t. mavortium

A. t. nebulosum
(intergrade)

TIGER SALAMANDER
to 13⅜ in. (338 mm)

A. t. melanostictum

A. t. diaboli

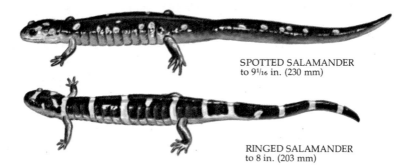

SPOTTED SALAMANDER
to 9¹/₁₆ in. (230 mm)

RINGED SALAMANDER
to 8 in. (203 mm)

MARBLED SALAMANDER
to 5 in. (127 mm)

recently
transformed

♀

SMALL-MOUTH SALAMANDER
to 9¼ in. (235 mm)

LONG-TOED SALAMANDER (*Ambystoma macrodactylum*). Found from sea level to altitudes of 9,000 ft., under debris in sagebrush desert to mountain meadows, always near lakes, pools, slow streams. Dark brown to black above, with light back stripe; dark brown to dirty white below. Has tubercles on feet, 12–13 costal grooves; appressed limbs overlap by up to 2 costal folds. Rare and endangered. Five subspecies: (1) *A. m. macrodactylum*—yellow or green stripe vaguely defined especially on head, sides white-flecked; (2) *A. m. columbianum*—tan to yellow stripe sharply defined but forming large patches on head; (3) *A. m. krausei*—greenish yellow stripe runs from snout down back; (4) *A. m. sigillatum*—vivid but discontinuous stripe commonly yellowish; (5) *A. m. croceum*—discontinuous orange or yellow stripe.

NORTHWESTERN SALAMANDER (*Ambystoma gracile*). Found close to water, sea level to 10,000 ft., under debris in weeds or grasslands. Adults are seldom seen. Skin glands form large oval swelling behind each eye and rounded rough ridge along upper edge of tail. Somewhat like Tiger (p. 84), but has no tubercles on feet. Appressed front and back limbs overlap by 6 costal folds. Two subspecies: (1) *A. g. gracile*—uniform dark brown above, 3 segments in 4th toe, 10–11 costal grooves; (2) *A. g. decorticatum*—same color but with irregular light flecks above, 4 segments in 4th toe, 11–12 costal grooves.

TALPID SALAMANDER (*Ambystoma talpoideum*). Found in burrows or under debris in forests. Broad head; short body showing 10–11 costal grooves; appressed limbs touch or overlap slightly. Sides and belly covered with irregular gray spots, smaller and fewer on belly.

MABEE'S SALAMANDER (*Ambystoma mabeei*). Frequents low bottomlands. Dark brown or black above, light brown to gray below. Has 13 costal grooves; 2 folds between appressed limbs. Many pale flecks on sides, fewer and smaller on back, few and scattered on belly.

FLATWOODS SALAMANDER (*Ambystoma cingulatum*). At home in slash pine and cypress swamps. Adults black. Costal grooves, 13–16, usually 15; 1–2 costal folds between appressed limbs. Commonly marked by mesh of fine gray lines on back and sides; network sometimes indistinct or absent. Dark below, usually gray-speckled.

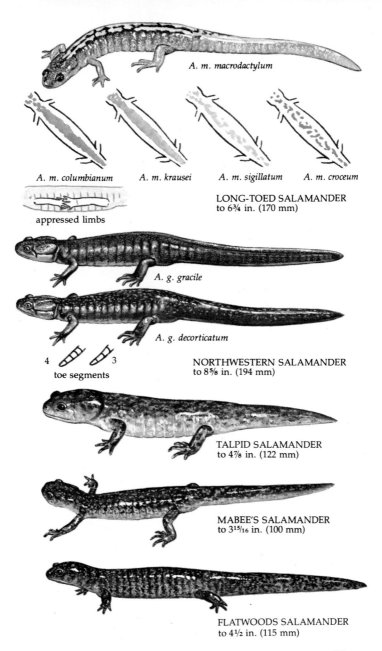

A. m. macrodactylum

A. m. columbianum   *A. m. krausei*   *A. m. sigillatum*   *A. m. croceum*

appressed limbs

LONG-TOED SALAMANDER
to 6¾ in. (170 mm)

A. g. gracile

A. g. decorticatum

4   3
toe segments

NORTHWESTERN SALAMANDER
to 8⅝ in. (194 mm)

TALPID SALAMANDER
to 4⅞ in. (122 mm)

MABEE'S SALAMANDER
to 3¹⁵/₁₆ in. (100 mm)

FLATWOODS SALAMANDER
to 4½ in. (115 mm)

87

JEFFERSONIANUM GROUP of mole salamanders consists of four unusual species. Many thousands of years ago, Jefferson's and Blue-spotted salamanders interbred, creating two hybrid species, Silvery and Tremblay's, both with three sets of chromosomes rather than the normal 2. One set is from one parent, two from the other. Silvery has two sets from Jefferson's; Tremblay's, two sets from Blue-spotted. Only one hybrid male (a Silvery) has ever been recorded. Silvery females mate with Jefferson's males, Tremblay's females with Blue-spotted males. The male's sperm activates the female's eggs, but the sperm nucleus with its hereditary material does not merge with the egg nucleus. Consequently, the offspring inherit characteristics only from the female. Each hybrid is largely confined to the range of the species with which it mates. It also occurs, however, in other small areas where only the second mating species occurs. In these cases, perhaps this second species may provide the egg-activating sperm, or perhaps the eggs need no activation in such areas.

Each hybrid species is so similar to the species with which it mates that distinguishing the two with certainty requires microscopic studies. But during the spring breeding season, mature males develop a swelling around the vent and thus can be distinguished from females and identified almost positively as either Jefferson's or Blue-spotted. Size, coloration, and distance between nostrils are also distinguishing features. All four species have 12 costal grooves. Some authorities regard the hybrid populations invalid as species, considering them only variants of the parent contributing the most chromosomes.

JEFFERSON'S SALAMANDER (*Ambystoma jeffersonianum*). Brown or gray above, paler below. Legs and sides commonly peppered with blue. Distance between nostrils: 3/16–1/4 in. (5.0–6. mm).

BLUE-SPOTTED SALAMANDER (*Ambystoma laterale*). Black or dark gray above, paler below. Many large pale blue flecks over entire body, especially along lower sides. Distance between nostrils: 3/32–5/32 in. (2.7–3.9 mm).

SILVERY SALAMANDER (*Ambystoma platineum*). A hybrid species. Brownish gray above, paler below. Bluish flecks scattered over top, upper sides; larger flecks on belly, lower sides. Distance between nostrils: 3/16–1/4 in. (4.6–6.0 mm).

TREMBLAY'S SALAMANDER (*Ambystoma tremblayi*). A hybrid species. Dark gray to gray-black above, lighter below. Many diffused bluish white marks especially along lower sides. Distance between nostrils: 1/8–3/16 in. 3.3–4.7 mm).

HOW HYBRIDS REPRODUCE

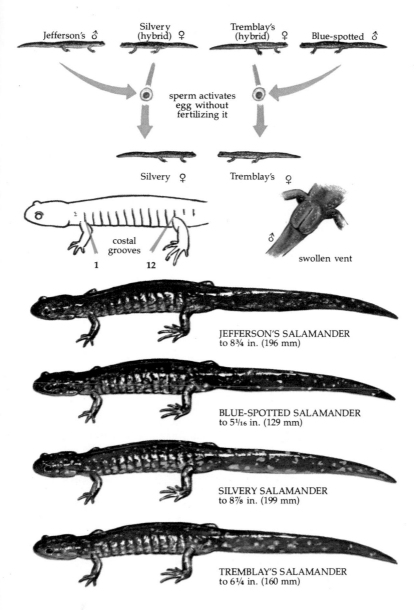

Jefferson's ♂   Silvery (hybrid) ♀   Tremblay's (hybrid) ♀   Blue-spotted ♂

sperm activates egg without fertilizing it

Silvery ♀   Tremblay's ♀

costal grooves
1   12

♂
swollen vent

JEFFERSON'S SALAMANDER
to 8¾ in. (196 mm)

BLUE-SPOTTED SALAMANDER
to 5¹/₁₆ in. (129 mm)

SILVERY SALAMANDER
to 8⅞ in. (199 mm)

TREMBLAY'S SALAMANDER
to 6¼ in. (160 mm)

LUNGLESS SALAMANDERS—family Plethodontidae

There are 15–16 genera and 77 species of lungless salamanders in the United States and Canada. These creatures breathe through the skin and the lining of the mouth. The lack of lungs is an ancestral adaptation to mountain streams, where some species still dwell. Lungs are buoyant, making it difficult for salamanders to hold fast in rushing water.

Adult lungless salamanders are unique in having a groove from lip to nostril. This nasolabial groove, often visible only with a hand lens, conducts substances to the nostril and thus aids olfaction. Two subfamilies: the Plethodontinae, including the Red Hills, Shovel-nosed (p. 126), and dusky salamanders (p. 92), have a fixed lower jaw; the Desmognathinae, other lungless salamanders, can move both jaws.

KEY TO LUNGLESS SALAMANDERS

1. Gills ....*see* **2**
   No gills ....*see* **3**
2. (*not shown*) 4 gill slits ....*see* **5**
   3 gill slits ....*see* **7**
3. Light line, eye to mouth ....*see* **5**
   No light line ....*see* **4**
4. Neck wider than head; eyes not protuberant ....*see* **5**
   Neck narrower or no wider than head; eyes protuberant......*see* **7**
5. 13–15 costal grooves ....*see* **6**
   20–22 grooves ...**Red Hills,** p. 126
6. Internal nostrils visible; light line from eye to mouth..................
   ....**dusky salamanders,** p. 92
   Not as above ....
   ....**Shovel-nosed,** p. 126
7. Pigmented body; normal-sized eyes ....*see* **8**
   Colorless body; tiny eyes ...**grotto** and **blind salamanders,** p. 106
8. 4 toes ....*see* **9**
   5 toes ....*see* **10**
9. (*not shown*) 13–14 costal grooves .... **Four-toed,** p. 128
   15–16 grooves ......**Dwarf,** p. 128
   17–22 (rarely 16) costal grooves .....**slender salamanders,** p. 110
10. (*not shown*) Gills ....*see* **11**
    No gills ....*see* **14**
11. (*not shown*) Pattern of longitudinal lines .....**Many-lined,** p. 126
    No such pattern ....*see* **12**
12. Found W of Mississippi ....
    brook salamanders, p. 98, or **grotto salamanders,** p. 106
    Found E of Mississippi ......*see* **13**

13. (*not shown*) Double row of light spots or broad light band on back..**brook salamanders,** p. 98
    Unicolored, darkly reticulated, or randomly dark back ....**red** and **spring salamanders,** p. 104
14. Tongue attached in front ..*see* **15**
    Attached in middle ....*see* **18**
15. Tail constricted near base ....
    ....**Ensatina,** p. 128
    Not constricted near base ....*see* **16**
16. Digits square-tipped; or teeth protruding below upper lip......
    ...**climbing salamanders,** p. 124
    Digits round-tipped; teeth not protruding ....*see* **17**
17. (*not shown*) Sensory pits on head, alternating light-dark lines on sides ....**Many-lined,** p. 126
    Not as above ....
    woodland salamanders, p. 114
18. Digits about half-webbed ....
    ..**web-toed salamanders,** p. 108
    Short webs or none ....*see* **19**
19. (*not shown*) Dark-bordered light line along sides of snout ......**spring salamanders,** p. 104
    No light line along snout ..*see* **20**
20. Found W of Mississippi ....
    ....**brook salamanders,** p. 98
    Found E of Mississippi ......*see* **21**
21. (*not shown*) 16 or more costal grooves; sides not darker than back ....**red salamanders,** p. 104
    15 or fewer costal grooves; or if more, sides darker than back ....**brook salamanders,** p. 98

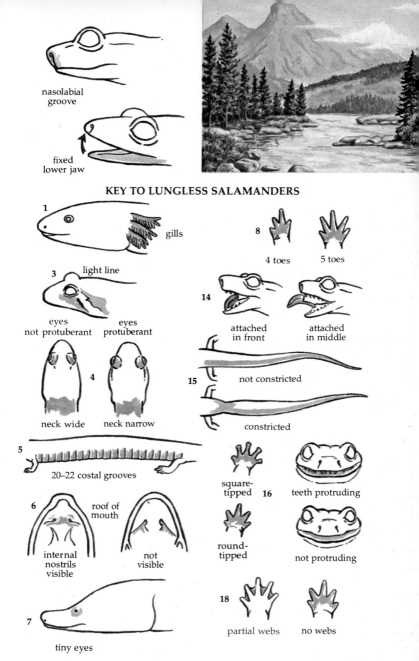

nasolabial groove

fixed lower jaw

KEY TO LUNGLESS SALAMANDERS

1 gills

3 light line

eyes not protuberant

eyes protuberant

4

neck wide

neck narrow

5 20–22 costal grooves

6 roof of mouth

internal nostrils visible

not visible

7 tiny eyes

8 4 toes 5 toes

14 attached in front

attached in middle

15 not constricted

constricted

16 square-tipped

teeth protruding

round-tipped

not protruding

18 partial webs no webs

91

DUSKY SALAMANDERS—genus *Desmognathus*

A light line from the eye to the corner of the mouth in most individuals distinguishes the duskies from other lungless salamanders. But dusky salamander species are difficult to tell from one another except sometimes by geographic range.

Eggs usually are laid under objects near water, sometimes under stones in water. After hatching, the larvae of all species except the Pigmy enter the water. Some adults live on land; others remain in the streams and breed there.

KEY TO DUSKY SALAMANDERS

1. Tail oval or circular in cross section, not keeled above ......*see* **2**
   Tail triangular in cross section, often keeled above ....*see* **4**
2. Herringbone pattern usually on back; tail less than half total length ....**Pigmy,** below
   No herringbone pattern; tail half total length or longer ....*see* **3**
3. Continuous dark line on upper sides ....**Mountain,** p. 96
   No continuous line ....
   ....**Cherokee,** p. 96
4. Belly of adults uniform deep brown or blue-black; belly of half-grown specimens dark but flecked with yellow; belly of youngest light ....
   ....**Black-bellied,** p. 96
   Bellies not as described ....*see* **5**
5. Belly of adults light, usually uniform in color; young with 4 pairs of orange-brown spots above; strong dark marks on back of older animals; costal grooves 13, rarely 14 ....
   ....**Seal,** p. 94

Belly of adults usually distinctly colored, often mottled or speckled; young with 5–8 pairs of yellowish spots above; back of adults mark-free or with marks confined to line along sides; costal grooves 14, rarely 15.......
   .... *see* **6**
6. Large light spots on back, narrowly spaced; usually 2–3, rarely 4½ costal folds between appressed limbs ....
   ....**Northern Dusky,** p. 94
   Small light spots on back, widely spaced; 4½–5½ costal folds between appressed limbs in specimens with snout-to-vent length of more than 1¾ in. (45 mm), no less than 3½ folds in smaller specimens ....
   ....**Southern Dusky,** p. 94

PIGMY SALAMANDER (*Desmognathus wrighti*). Smallest dusky salamander and the only one that has no aquatic larval stage. Eggs, laid in seepage, hatch into transformed young; these lack gills, resemble mature individuals. Adults stay on land, living at elevations of 3,500–6,500 ft. Back marked by light tan to red stripe; sides dark, belly lighter-hued. Small size, a tail less than half the animal's total length, and usually a striking gray-to-black crosshatching on back distinguish Pigmy from other dusky salamanders.

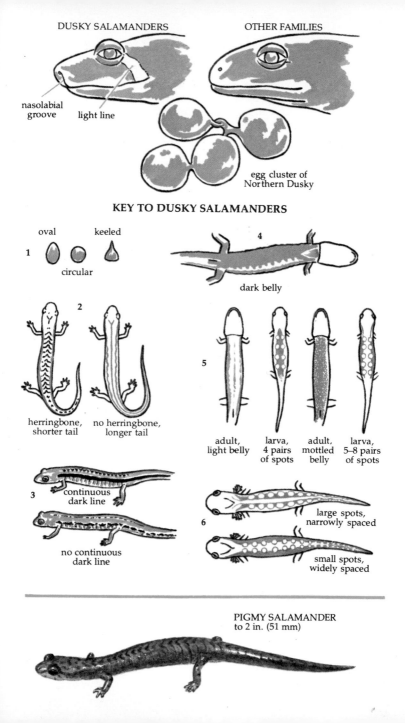

DUSKY SALAMANDERS · OTHER FAMILIES

nasolabial groove · light line

egg cluster of Northern Dusky

KEY TO DUSKY SALAMANDERS

1 · oval · keeled · circular

4 · dark belly

2 · herringbone, shorter tail · no herringbone, longer tail

5 · adult, light belly · larva, 4 pairs of spots · adult, mottled belly · larva, 5–8 pairs of spots

3 · continuous dark line · no continuous dark line

6 · large spots, narrowly spaced · small spots, widely spaced

PIGMY SALAMANDER
to 2 in. (51 mm)

NORTHERN DUSKY SALAMANDER (*Desmognathus fuscus*). Adults of this species live on land or in water. Dark tan to brown on back and sides. Along upper portion of each side extends a row of large yellowish spots as wide as or wider than the spaces between, but aged males may lack the spots and be almost uniformly dark above. Color of belly varies. Tail somewhat less than half the animal's total length. Costal grooves number 14, rarely 15; costal folds between appressed limbs, usually 2–3, rarely to 4½. Larvae have 9–17 pigmentless terminal gill filaments per side. Three subspecies: (1) *D. f. fuscus* (includes *D. planiceps*)—belly slightly mottled but mostly unmarked, light spots on back fused into distinct shallow-toothed band; (2) *D. f. conanti*—belly extensively mottled, light spots on back separate or fused into deeply toothed band; (3) *D. f. welteri* (now considered a full species by most authorities)—belly lightly mottled, back mottled and usually lacking light-colored band.

SOUTHERN DUSKY SALAMANDER (*Desmognathus auriculatus*). Either terrestrial or aquatic during adult life. Almost uniformly dark back and sides; no pattern, or a row of widely spaced light dots, along upper sides. Belly commonly dark, but varies. Tail slightly less than half total body length. Costal grooves number 14, rarely 15; 4½–5½ costal folds between appressed limbs in larger specimens, and no less than 3½ folds in smaller specimens. Larvae have 22–40 pigmented and pendant gill filaments per side. Two subspecies (regarded as separate species by some authorities): (1) *D. a. auriculatus* (includes *D. a. carri*)—7–9 light-colored spots on back between front and back limbs; (2) *D. a. brimleyorum*—11–14 pale spots on back between front and hind limbs.

SEAL SALAMANDER (*Desmognathus monticola*). Terrestrial as adults. Brown back with light buff to gray-brown markings, which sometimes fuse into a wavy stripe on tail, are black-bordered on the sides. Belly white in young, light gray or tan in adults; usually uniform, sometimes mottled. Tail about half the animal's total length, terminates in a sharp top edge. Two subspecies: (1) *D. m. monticola*—black bordered light spots on back form a coarse network; (2) *D. m. jeffersoni*—scattered eye-sized dark spots on back.

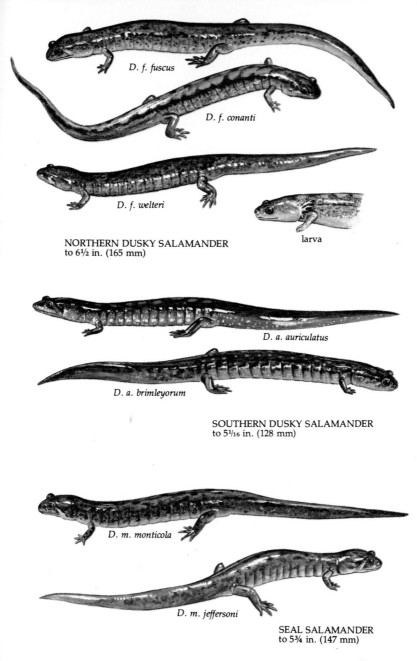

D. f. fuscus

D. f. conanti

D. f. welteri

larva

NORTHERN DUSKY SALAMANDER
to 6½ in. (165 mm)

D. a. auriculatus

D. a. brimleyorum

SOUTHERN DUSKY SALAMANDER
to 5¹/₁₆ in. (128 mm)

D. m. monticola

D. m. jeffersoni

SEAL SALAMANDER
to 5¾ in. (147 mm)

MOUNTAIN SALAMANDER *(Desmognathus ochrophaeus)*. Adults are terrestrial, often found under logs, rocks, and other debris where moisture gathers. These salamanders vary greatly in color: sometimes almost uniformly dark, more often with a lighter stripe of yellow, red, brown, or gray running down back. Stripe has dark borders, frequently dark dots or line of **V**'s down middle. Limbs, cheeks, and certain other body parts sometimes paler or reddish. Belly finely marked with black. Rounded tail accounts for half or more of animal's total length. Has 13–15, usually 14, costal grooves, 2–5 grooves between appressed front and back limbs. Two subspecies are commonly recognized, though not by all authorities: (1) *D. o. ochrophaeus*—light stripe on back has straight edges; (2) *D. o. carolinensis*—light stripe on back has curving or undulating edges. *D. imitator,* the Imitator Salamander, has recently been segregated from *D. ochrophaeus;* both inhabit the Smoky Mts. of North Carolina and Tennessee. *D. imitator* can often be recognized by its reddish cheeks, mimicking those of Jordan's Salamander (p. 122).

BLACK-BELLIED SALAMANDER *(Desmognathus quadramaculatus)*. This is the largest of the dusky salamanders. Lives in mountain streams throughout life—the only dusky salamander always aquatic. Adults are usually black all over or nearly so; belly may be dark brown. Usually two prominent lines of light spots run along sides. Young somewhat lighter in color, and yellow-flecked on belly; some have a strikingly light-colored head. Tail has a sharp upper edge, accounts for less than half the animal's total length. Costal grooves, 14; 2 or 3 grooves between appressed front and hind limbs.

CHEROKEE SALAMANDER *(Desmognathus aeneus)*. Adults are terrestrial, living under debris in damp places. Wide reddish, yellow, or tan stripe runs along back, with dark dots or blotches or with a continuous dark median line. Sides dark fading to a pale or mottled brown-and-white belly. Tail rounded and accounts for at least half the animal's total length. This salamander has 13–14 costal grooves, 3–5 grooves between appressed front and back limbs. Two subspecies (not accepted by all authorities): (1) *D. a. aeneus*—edges of back stripe are straight; (2) *D. a. chermocki*—edges of stripe wavy.

young

D. o. ochrophaeus

D. o. carolinensis

MOUNTAIN SALAMANDER
to 4⅜ in. (112 mm)

BLACK-BELLIED SALAMANDER
to 7⅝ in. (193 mm)

D. a. aeneus

D. a. chermocki

CHEROKEE SALAMANDER
to 2⁵⁄₁₆ in. (58 mm)

BROOK SALAMANDERS—genus *Eurycea*

This extremely diverse group of lungless salamanders includes some species that are neotenic—that is, they retain the gills and remain in the larval form throughout life. Some are cave dwellers with little or no sight and no skin color. The maximum total length varies from 2 to 7¼ in., according to species. Three distinct groups should probably be recognized as subgenera: long-bodied, central Texas, and eastern.

KEY TO BROOK SALAMANDERS

1. 19 or more costal grooves ....*see* **6**
   17 or fewer costal grooves ....*see* **2**
2. Found only in central Texas ..*see* **8**
   Not found in Texas, or found at extreme NE border only ....*see* **3**
3. Tail less than half total length ......
   ...... **Cumberland Brook,** p. 102
   Tail more than half total length
   ....*see* **4**
4. 0–2 costal grooves between appressed limbs ....*see* **5**
   3–5 costal grooves between appressed limbs ....
   ....**Two-lined,** p. 102
5. Dark vertical bars on tail of transformed adults ....
   ....**Long-tailed,** p. 102
   No dark vertical bars on tail ....
   .... **Cave,** p. 102
6. (*not shown*) Gills ....*see* **7**
   No gills ......**Many-ribbed,** p. 100

7. (*not shown*) Yellowish with scattered dark granules on belly
   ...**Many-ribbed** (larval forms), p. 100
   Not yellowish; uncolored belly
   ....**Oklahoma,** below
8. Eyes small, diameter one-fourth to one-third distance between them ....*see* **9**
   Eyes large, diameter one-half or more distance between them
   ....*see* **10**
9. Eyes partly or wholly covered with skin ....
   ....**Valdina Farms,** p. 100
   Eyes not covered with skin ....
   ....**Cascade Cave,** p. 100
10. Dark ring at margin of pupil ....
    ....**San Marcos,** p. 100
    No dark ring ....**Texas,** p. 100

LONG-BODIED GROUP of brook salamanders consists of two species with 19 or more costal grooves—17 is the maximum for other brook salamanders. Gilled specimens can be distinguished from the Grotto Salamander (p. 106) only by slightly larger eyes, more color (in some), and geographic range. The long-bodied group is limited to Ouachita and Ozark uplifts, the Grotto Salamander to Ozark uplift.

OKLAHOMA SALAMANDER (*Eurycea tynerensis*). Found in cool spring-fed gravel-bottomed streams, usually below 1,000 ft., in drainage systems of Grand and Illinois rivers. Retains gills throughout life. Back gray with black spots, streaks, or network. Belly uncolored. Tail somewhat less than half the animal's total length. Has 19–21 costal grooves, 7–11 between appressed front and back limbs.

KEY TO BROOK SALAMANDERS

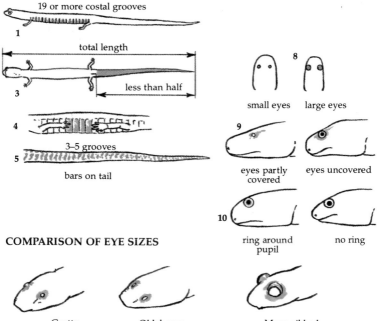

19 or more costal grooves

1

total length

3

less than half

4

5   3–5 grooves

bars on tail

COMPARISON OF EYE SIZES

8

small eyes   large eyes

9

eyes partly   eyes uncovered
covered

10

ring around   no ring
pupil

Grotto   Oklahoma   Many-ribbed

OKLAHOMA SALAMANDER
to 3⅛ in. (80 mm)

MANY-RIBBED SALAMANDER (*Eurycea multiplicata*). Lives under stones and debris in shallow streams and springs, sometimes in caves, occasionally on land. Transformed adults and larvae about to transform have a broad brown band down middle of back, darker sides, and a pale gray to yellow belly with or without scattered dark pigment. Some have yellow above and below. Young larvae and large neotenic specimens are pale gray to yellowish, stippled with dark gray. Long slender body has 19–20 costal grooves. Two subspecies: (1) *E. m. multiplicata*—never neotenic, belly with few or no dark granules; (2) *E. m. griseogaster*—sometimes neotenic, belly with many dark granules.

CENTRAL TEXAS GROUP of brook salamanders is limited to waters of caves, sinkholes, springs, and underground channels of the southern eroded edge of the Edwards Plateau in Texas. All species are neotenic. Since ranges rarely overlap, the site of observation or collection is important in identification.

TEXAS SALAMANDER (*Eurycea neotenes*). Brown-speckled yellowish hues above; sides carry 1 or 2 lines of pale spots; belly pale. Has 15–17 costal grooves. Two subspecies: (1) *E. n. neotenes*—embraces range of whole group, from Val Verde County to Williamson County; (2) *E. n. pterophila*—sole verified habitat is Fern Back Spring, Wimberley, Hays County.

SAN MARCOS SALAMANDER (*Eurycea nana*). Occurs in Comal Springs area, San Marcos, Hays County. Characteristically the back is a gray-brown; 2 rows of 7–9 small irregular pale spots run along back; belly white. Has 16–17 costal grooves.

CASCADE CAVE SALAMANDER (*Eurycea latitans*). Named after cave in which it occurs, near Boerne, Kendall County. Back is pale cream mottled with brown; distinct white flecks appear on sides and tail. Eyes are lidless. Costal grooves, 14–15.

VALDINA FARMS SALAMANDER (*Eurycea troglodytes*). Known only from Valdina Farms Sinkhole, 16 miles N of D'Hanis, Medina County. Pale cream to light gray above, indistinctly flecked or streaked with white or yellow. Lower sides and belly are colorless. Usually 13 costal grooves, sometimes 14.

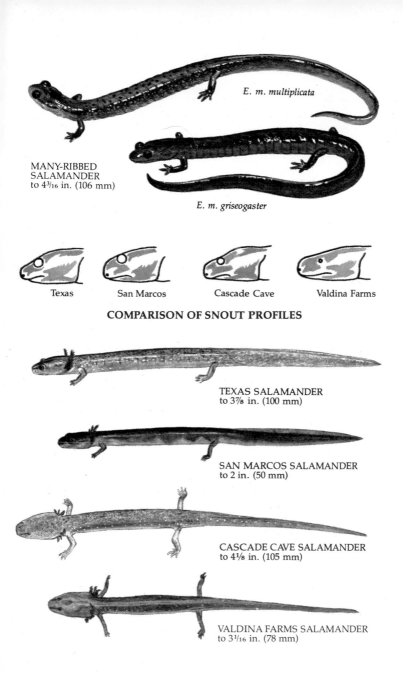

E. m. multiplicata

MANY-RIBBED
SALAMANDER
to 4³/₁₆ in. (106 mm)

E. m. griseogaster

| Texas | San Marcos | Cascade Cave | Valdina Farms |

COMPARISON OF SNOUT PROFILES

TEXAS SALAMANDER
to 3⅞ in. (100 mm)

SAN MARCOS SALAMANDER
to 2 in. (50 mm)

CASCADE CAVE SALAMANDER
to 4⅛ in. (105 mm)

VALDINA FARMS SALAMANDER
to 3¹/₁₆ in. (78 mm)

EASTERN GROUP of brook salamanders includes five species bearing 13–16 costal grooves. Never neotenic.

TWO-LINED SALAMANDER (*Eurycea bislineata*). Frequents streams, and swamps. Four subspecies: (1) *E. b. bislineata*—15–16 costal grooves; (2) *E. b. cirrigera*—13–14 costal grooves, 2 grooves between tips of appressed limbs, brown stripe to tip or last quarter of tail; (3) *E. b. rivicola*—13–14 costal grooves, 3 between appressed limbs; (4) *E. b. wilderae*—13–14 costal grooves, 2 between appressed limbs, black stripe runs halfway into tail.

JUNALUSKA TWO-LINED SALAMANDER (*Eurycea junaluska*). Recently registered in Graham Co., North Carolina. Yellow or orange back with numerous dim dark dots or flecks on tail. [Not illustrated.]

LONG-TAILED SALAMANDER (*Eurycea longicauda*). Lives largely on land in moist places. Has a longer tail (58–67 percent of total body length) than Two-lined. Dark vertical bars on tail distinguish Long-tailed from Cave Salamander. Long-tailed adults are distinguishable by a light yellowish-brown band with dark markings down the back, a dark band on each side, and a white belly. Costal grooves number 14. Three subspecies: (1) *E. l. longicauda*—belly unmarked; (2) *E. l. guttolineata*—black line bordered by light tan or yellow line down middle of back; (3) *E. l. melanopleura*—belly mottled.

CAVE SALAMANDER (*Eurycea lucifuga*). Terrestrial; frequents caves and wooded margins of caves; sometimes found in swampy areas. Light red hues above, occasionally yellow; dark patches mark back, sides, and tail. Belly pale yellow to colorless, usually unmarked. Tail is longer (58–67 percent of total body length) than that of Two-lined. Costal grooves, 14–15.

CUMBERLAND BROOK SALAMANDER (*Eurycea aquatica*). Lives in cool, gravel-bottomed, spring-fed streams, among watercress. Only member of eastern group with a tail less than 50 percent of animal's total length. In transformed individuals, back bears a broad brownish band, sides are black, belly is lightly stippled or uncolored. Costal grooves, 13. Reliably known only near Bessemer, Alabama, but may occur in N Alabama, NW Georgia, SW Tennessee, NE Mississippi.

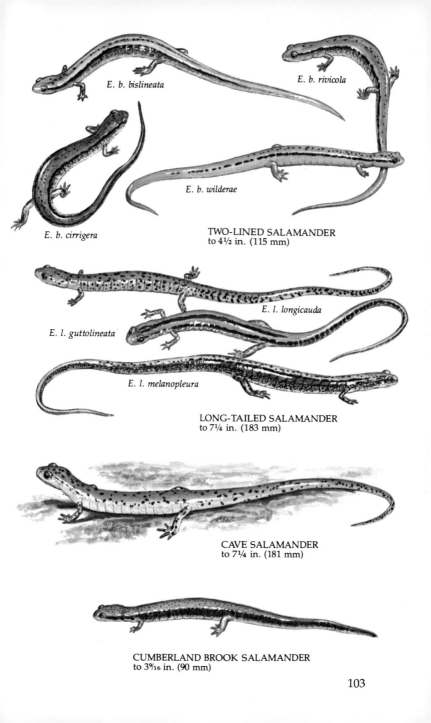

E. b. bislineata

E. b. rivicola

E. b. cirrigera

E. b. wilderae

TWO-LINED SALAMANDER
to 4½ in. (115 mm)

E. l. guttolineata

E. l. longicauda

E. l. melanopleura

LONG-TAILED SALAMANDER
to 7¼ in. (183 mm)

CAVE SALAMANDER
to 7¼ in. (181 mm)

CUMBERLAND BROOK SALAMANDER
to 3⁹/₁₆ in. (90 mm)

103

RED AND SPRING SALAMANDERS
—genera *Pseudotriton* and *Gyrinophilus*

These five similar salamanders are sometimes included in one genus—*Pseudotriton*. The larvae of all but the Tennessee Cave Salamander lose their gills and breed only in the transformed state.

RED SALAMANDER (*Pseudotriton ruber*). Found in clear cool springs and streams or under nearby debris. Eyes usually yellow. Four subspecies: (1) *P. r. ruber*—spots with diffuse edges, legs and tail unspotted below; (2) *P. r. vioscai*—spots with diffuse edges, legs and tail black-flecked below; (3) *P. r. nitidus*—sharp-edged spots ending halfway to tail tip; (4) *P. r. schencki*—sharp-edged spots nearly to tip of tail.

MUD SALAMANDER (*Pseudotriton montanus*). Found under stones and logs in muddy places near water. Varies from red to brown, usually reddish above. Eyes brownish. Snout shorter than Red's. Four subspecies differing in number of costal grooves and belly spotting: (1) *P. m. montanus*—17 grooves, belly spotted; (2) *P. m. diastictus*—unspotted; (3) *P. m. flavissimus*—16, unspotted; (4) *P. m. floridanus*—18, unspotted.

SPRING SALAMANDER (*Gyrinophilus porphyriticus*) Found in or along clear upland streams, springs, caves. Often cannibalistic. Unique dark-bordered light line from eye to nostril distinguishes adults from other reddish salamanders. Four subspecies: (1) *G. p. porphyriticus*—dark spots or netlike marks on back; (2) *G. p. duryi*—dim eye-nostril line, few dark marks on back; (3) *G. p. dunni*—darkly speckled back; (4) *G. p. danielsi*—many black dots on back.

WEST VIRGINIA SPRING SALAMANDER (*Gyrinophilus subterraneus*). Small eyes, gray network on pale back. Recently described, from General Davis Cave, NE of Alderson, West Virginia. [Not illustrated.]

TENNESSEE CAVE SALAMANDER (*Gyrinophilus palleucus*). Neotenic in cave waters. Eyes are small, snout broad and turned up at tip. Nearly white to dark brown. Three subspecies: (1) *G. p. palleucus*—nearly white; (2) *G. p. gulolineatus*—dark brown above, dark stripe on middle of throat; (3) *G. p. necturoides*—dark brown above, no stripe on throat.

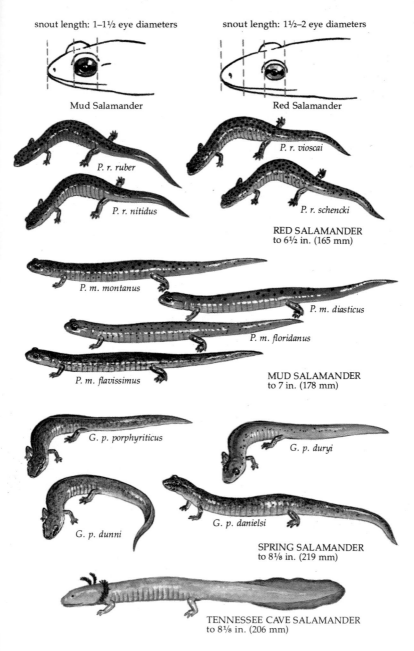

snout length: 1–1½ eye diameters

snout length: 1½–2 eye diameters

Mud Salamander

Red Salamander

P. r. ruber

P. r. nitidus

P. r. vioscai

P. r. schencki

RED SALAMANDER
to 6½ in. (165 mm)

P. m. montanus

P. m. diasticus

P. m. floridanus

P. m. flavissimus

MUD SALAMANDER
to 7 in. (178 mm)

G. p. porphyriticus

G. p. duryi

G. p. dunni

G. p. danielsi

SPRING SALAMANDER
to 8⅛ in. (219 mm)

TENNESSEE CAVE SALAMANDER
to 8⅛ in. (206 mm)

105

GROTTO AND BLIND SALAMANDERS
—genera *Typhlotriton, Typhlomolge,* and *Haideotriton*

These salamanders live mostly or entirely in cave or subterranean waters. The only other true cave-dwelling salamanders of North America are some species of brook and spring salamanders. (Elsewhere in the world, the only species of similar habits is the famous Olm, *Proteus anguinus,* of Europe.) The three North American genera evolved independently from different ancestors but have converged—that is, have developed similar characteristics as a result of their common, highly restrictive environment. They tend to have degenerate eyes and to be extremely slender, pale-colored, and wraithlike. They survive on little food, presumably found largely by the sense of smell; some food particles may be absorbed through the skin. The Grotto is long-bodied, has 17–20 costal grooves; the other three species are short-bodied, have 12–13 costal grooves. Some authorities place one (*T. rathbuni*) or both *Typhlomolge* species in the genus *Eurycea.*

KEY TO GROTTO AND BLIND SALAMANDERS

1. 17–20 costal grooves; normal-sized legs; clearly visible eyes ... .**Grotto,** below
   12–13 grooves; thin legs; tiny or no eye spots ....*see* **2**
2. Sides of head nearly parallel; eyes scarcely visible or not at all; neck narrower than body......... ....**Georgia Blind,** below

   Sides of head taper toward snout; eyes tiny but clearly visible; neck not narrower than body ... .*see* **3**
3. Limbs overlap 1–4 costal grooves; snout concave in front of eyes .. ..**Trident Blind,** p. 108
   Limbs overlap 6 grooves; snout flat in front of eyes ....**San Marcos Blind,** p. 108

 **GROTTO SALAMANDER** (*Typhlotriton spelaeus*). Inhabits caves and streams or pools nearby. Only species of this group that ever transforms; it does so only in caves and underground streams. Gills are lost, eyes degenerate and become almost useless, and body loses most of color. Larvae—with plum, brown, or pearl hues on back and sides—live mostly in springs and streams in the open. They resemble larvae of Oklahoma (p. 98) and Many-ribbed (p. 100) salamanders. Smaller eyes, uniform color, and often fewer costal grooves help distinguish Grotto larvae from those of other species.

 GEORGIA BLIND SALAMANDER (*Haideotriton wallacei*). Found only in artesian and cave waters. White with scattered coloring, elongated reddish gills. Eyes not visible or barely so. Costal grooves, 12–13, with 1 or 2 in overlap of appressed limbs.

KEY TO GROTTO AND BLIND SALAMANDERS

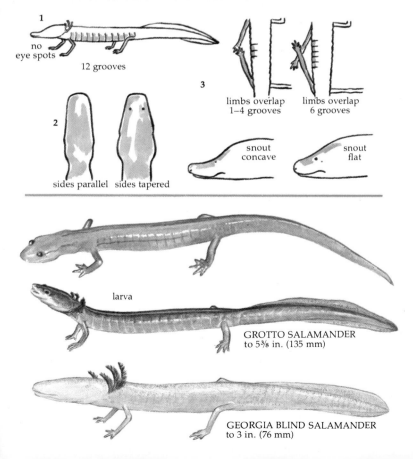

1

no eye spots

12 grooves

2

sides parallel   sides tapered

3

limbs overlap 1–4 grooves   limbs overlap 6 grooves

snout concave   snout flat

larva

GROTTO SALAMANDER
to 5⅜ in. (135 mm)

GEORGIA BLIND SALAMANDER
to 3 in. (76 mm)

TRIDENT BLIND SALAMANDER (*Typhlomolge tridentifera*). Known only from a stream in Honey Creek Cave, Comal County, Texas. Similar to cave-dwelling brook salamanders, but always has 12 costal grooves (rather than 13–17). Long slender limbs overlap when appressed (rare in brook salamanders). Snout flatter than in brook salamanders. Tridents never transform. Body white, with sparse dark pigment. Eyes tiny, snout concave in front of eyes.

SAN MARCOS BLIND SALAMANDER (*Typhlomolge rathbuni*). Found only in cave streams and artesian wells. Similar to Trident Blind, but has smaller eyes—mere black dots. Body white, with sparse dark pigment. Snout flat in front of eyes. Rare and endangered.

WEB-TOED SALAMANDERS—genus *Hydromantes*

All species of Hydromantes are distinguishable by the webs between the toes, a tail much shorter than the rest of the body, and 13 costal grooves. Also, the tongue is longer and attached by a central stalk. Eggs are laid on land; young have no aquatic larval stage.

SHASTA SALAMANDER (*Hydromantes shastae*). Found south of Mt. Shasta near headwaters of Shasta Reservoir, California. Favors limestone caves and fissures within forests, 1,000–2,500 ft. Color ranges from reddish brown to gray-green; dark mottling above, white blotches below. Tail grading to yellow-orange.

MOUNT LYELL SALAMANDER (*Hydromantes platycephalus*). Found on north-facing slopes of Sierra Nevada between Sonora Pass and Twin Lakes, California. Lives at 3,600–10,800 ft., in crevices of granite cliffs or rock slides, near cave openings, melting snow, and spray zone of waterfalls. Deep brown to black above, with lichenlike flecks of greenish yellow to clay; dark below, with silvery spots on lower sides. Young are greenish. Head and body are flattened.

LIMESTONE SALAMANDER (*Hydromantes brunus*). Found at 1,100–2,500 ft. in pine-chaparral forest where Bear Creek meets Merced River, California. Prefers crevices of mossy limestone cliffs, rock slides. Adults—back solid brown, belly cream to tan, rarely with light spots. Young—vivid yellow-green, becoming pale yellow.

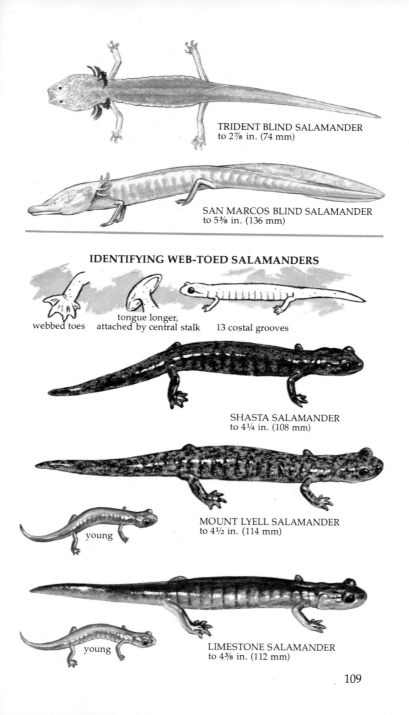

TRIDENT BLIND SALAMANDER
to 2⅞ in. (74 mm)

SAN MARCOS BLIND SALAMANDER
to 5⅜ in. (136 mm)

IDENTIFYING WEB-TOED SALAMANDERS

webbed toes

tongue longer,
attached by central stalk

13 costal grooves

SHASTA SALAMANDER
to 4¼ in. (108 mm)

young

MOUNT LYELL SALAMANDER
to 4½ in. (114 mm)

young

LIMESTONE SALAMANDER
to 4⅜ in. (112 mm)

SLENDER SALAMANDERS—genus *Batrachoseps*

These wormlike salamanders have a relatively long tail, four rear toes (rather than five), and a tongue supported by a central stalk. Seen mostly during the rainy season, November–May, they live under debris and in rotten logs at altitudes to 8,000 ft. When disturbed, they flip about wildly. Eggs are laid in moist places. The young do not go through an aquatic larval stage.

KEY TO SLENDER SALAMANDERS

1. Large white patches on sides of belly ....**Oregon,** below
White dots on sides of belly .. *see* **2**
2. Pale belly with dark spots .....*see* **3**
Dark belly with white dots ....*see* **4**
3. Snout-to-vent length more than 19 times width of hind foot......
.......................**Garden,** p. 112
Less than 19 times ....
...........**Channel Islands,** p. 112
4. (*not shown*) Underside of tail much paler than belly ....
........................**Desert,** below
Little paler or same ....*see* **5**

5. Snout-to-vent   length   6¹/₄–7¹/₄ times length of hind leg ....
...................**California,** p. 112
Snout-to-vent length 4¹/₂–6 times length of hind leg ....*see* **6**
6. 4–5 costal folds overlapped by appressed hind leg ....
.....................**Relictual,** p. 112
5–6¹/₂ costal folds overlapped by appressed hind leg ....*see* **7**
7. 18–19 costal grooves ....
......**Tehachapi** or **Desert,** below
20–21 costal grooves ....
..............**Kern Canyon,** p. 112

OREGON SLENDER SALAMANDER (*Batrachoseps wrighti*). Found under surface debris in damp forests to 3,000 ft. Yellow, tan, or red band, brightest at base of tail, runs down blackish brown back. Pale patches mark dark belly. Costal grooves, 16–17; 6–7 costal folds between appressed limbs.

DESERT SLENDER SALAMANDER (*Batrachoseps aridus*). Restricted to seepages in Hidden Palm Canyon (2,500 ft.), 10.5 miles S of Palm Desert, California. Pale flesh color; indistinct dorsal band of silver to orange flecks extending four-fifths length of tail; silver flecks on throat and chin; tail flesh-colored below. Costal grooves 16–19; snout-to-vent length 5¹/₂–7¹/₂ times head width. Rare and endangered.

TEHACHAPI SLENDER SALAMANDER (*Batrachoseps stebbinsi*). Found at 2,500–3,000 ft., 3 miles W of Paris Loraine in Piute Mts. and 6.3 miles SE of Keene in Tehachapi Mts., California. Has indistinct dorsal band of red, dark brown, or beige patches. Many white dots on undersides except mid-belly. Costal grooves, 18–19; 6–7 folds between appressed limbs.

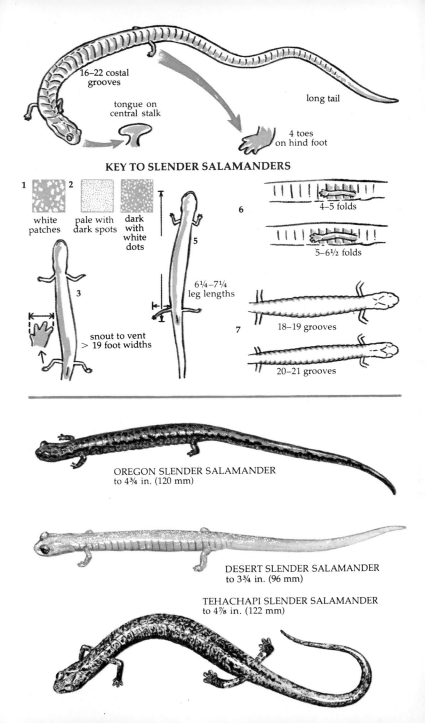

16–22 costal grooves

tongue on central stalk

long tail

4 toes on hind foot

KEY TO SLENDER SALAMANDERS

1 white patches

2 pale with dark spots

dark with white dots

3 snout to vent > 19 foot widths

5 6¼–7¼ leg lengths

6 4–5 folds

5–6½ folds

7 18–19 grooves

20–21 grooves

OREGON SLENDER SALAMANDER
to 4¾ in. (120 mm)

DESERT SLENDER SALAMANDER
to 3¾ in. (96 mm)

TEHACHAPI SLENDER SALAMANDER
to 4⅞ in. (122 mm)

CHANNEL ISLANDS SLENDER SALAMANDER (*Batrachoseps pacificus*). Light brown to dark or reddish brown above, pale with dark and white dots below. Snout and top of tail are often reddish. Young may have reddish back stripe and uniformly dark belly. Costal grooves, 17–20; 5½–8 folds between appressed limbs. Snout-to-vent length is 7–8 times head width.

GARDEN SLENDER SALAMANDER (*Batrachoseps major*). Found to 2,700 ft. Looks much like Channel Islands but snout-to-vent length is 8–9 times head width. Has 18–21 costal grooves, 9–12 costal folds between appressed limbs, 4–5½ folds overlapped by hind leg.

KERN CANYON SLENDER SALAMANDER (*Batrachoseps simatus*). Lives at 1,500–3,500 ft. on S side of Kern River Canyon and near Fairview, California. Light reddish-brown patches on back sometimes form indistinct band. Many tiny white dots below. Has 7½–9 costal folds between appressed limbs, 5½–6 folds overlapped by hind leg. Snout-to-vent length is 8–9 times head width.

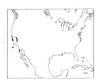

RELICTUAL SLENDER SALAMANDER (*Batrachoseps relictus*). Found in Sierra Nevada, Kern to Mariposa counties, 600–8,000 ft.; W Monterrey and N San Luis Obispo counties, 0–4,000 ft.; Santa Cruz Island, 0–700 ft.; Sierra San Pedro Mártir (Baja California), 7,000 ft. Pine-oak and chaparral habitats, often but not always near isolated brooks or seepages. Yellow, brown, red, or black-brown band along back; black sides; black or gray belly with white dots. Costal grooves, 16–20; 7–9½ costal folds between appressed limbs, 4–5 overlapped by appressed hind leg. Snout-to-vent length is 7½–8½ times head width.

CALIFORNIA SLENDER SALAMANDER (*Batrachoseps attenuatus*). Has a broad, black-edged, yellowish-brown to red stripe down back. Sides brown or gray stippled with white; darker belly bears fine white dots. Costal grooves, 18–21; 8–12½ costal folds between appressed limbs; 3½–4½ folds overlapped by appressed hind limb. Snout-to-vent length is 8½–10 times head width. *B. nigriventris*, the Black-bellied Slender Salamander, inhabiting southern half of range, is now considered a separate species.

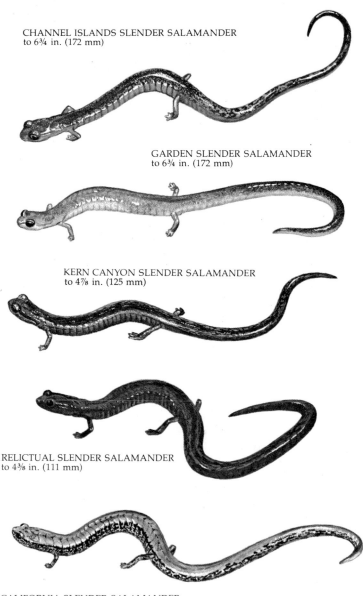

CHANNEL ISLANDS SLENDER SALAMANDER
to 6¾ in. (172 mm)

GARDEN SLENDER SALAMANDER
to 6¾ in. (172 mm)

KERN CANYON SLENDER SALAMANDER
to 4⅞ in. (125 mm)

RELICTUAL SLENDER SALAMANDER
to 4⅜ in. (111 mm)

CALIFORNIA SLENDER SALAMANDER
to 5⅜ in. (136 mm)

WOODLAND SALAMANDERS—genus *Plethodon*

With 24 species, this is the largest genus of salamanders north of Mexico. Its members have no striking features; they are recognized chiefly by the lack of features found in other salamanders. Most woodland species are medium-sized; none attain lengths of more than 7½ in. They have the usual five toes on each hind foot. They hatch from eggs laid on land in moist woods, omitting the aquatic larval stage common to most salamanders. The woodlands comprise four groups: the far western, the New Mexican, the slender eastern, and the robust eastern.

114

KEY TO WOODLAND SALAMANDERS

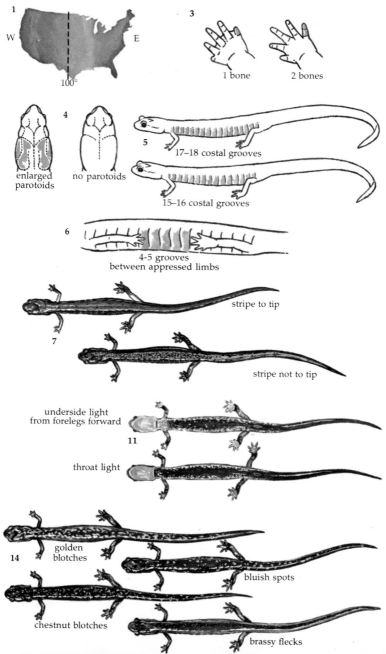

1

W   E

100°

3

1 bone   2 bones

4

enlarged parotoids   no parotoids

5

17–18 costal grooves

15–16 costal grooves

6

4-5 grooves between appressed limbs

7

stripe to tip

stripe not to tip

11

underside light from forelegs forward

throat light

14

golden blotches

bluish spots

chestnut blotches

brassy flecks

FAR WESTERN GROUP of woodland salamanders includes seven species. Most have a pale stripe running down the back.

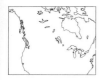

VAN DYKE'S SALAMANDER (*Plethodon vandykei*). Found under debris near water. Only woodland species with parotoid glands and 13–14 costal grooves. Usually tan, yellow, or orange back stripe but some adults covered entirely by one of those colors; dark sides and belly, yellow throat. Toes somewhat webbed. Two subspecies: (1) *P. v. vandykei*—dorsal stripe even-edged; (2) *P. v. idahoensis* (considered by some a full species, the Coeur d'Alêne Salamander)—edges of dorsal stripes scalloped.

LARCH MOUNTAIN SALAMANDER (*Plethodon larselli*). Lives in rotten wood and under rocks and bark among dense Douglas fir of Columbia River gorge. Tan, yellow, or pale red back stripe; black sides; red to coral belly. Costal grooves, 14–16, usually 15. Toes somewhat webbed, 5th toe very short.

DUNN'S SALAMANDER (*Plethodon dunni*). Favors trickles from streams, ponds and culverts in wooded areas. Usually greenish but sometimes yellowish back stripe, often darkly spotted, ends before tail tip. Belly slate with tiny yellow dots. Costal grooves, 14–16.

WESTERN RED-BACKED SALAMANDER (*Plethodon vehiculum*). Lives under debris in damp wooded areas. Back stripe yellow to orange, red, or brown. Sides dark; belly slate to blue, sometimes heavily patterned with random yellow to red markings. Adults may be uniformly yellowish or orange instead of striped. Costal grooves, 15–17, usually 16.

DEL NORTE SALAMANDER (*Plethodon elongatus*). Inhabits humid rocky areas. Young have reddish-brown back stripe that tends to be obliterated by brown or black as individual ages. Belly very dark, with a few white dots. Short toes, webbing not full. Costal grooves, 17–19.

SISKIYOU MOUNTAIN SALAMANDER (*Plethodon stormi*). Inhabits humid rocky areas. Resembles Del Norte, but young lack reddish stripe. Body dark brown, with pale dots above. Costal grooves, 17–18, usually 17.

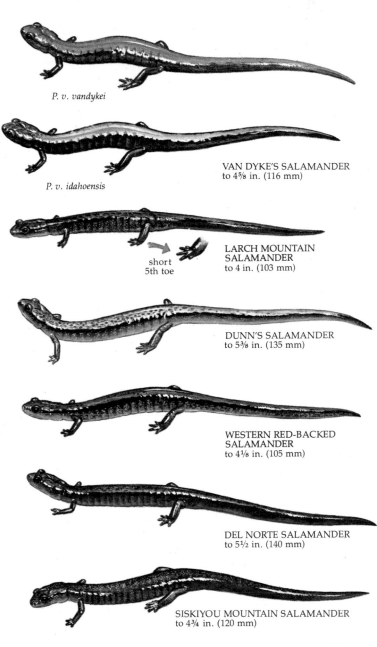

P. v. vandykei

P. v. idahoensis

VAN DYKE'S SALAMANDER
to 4⅝ in. (116 mm)

short
5th toe

LARCH MOUNTAIN
SALAMANDER
to 4 in. (103 mm)

DUNN'S SALAMANDER
to 5⅜ in. (135 mm)

WESTERN RED-BACKED
SALAMANDER
to 4⅛ in. (105 mm)

DEL NORTE SALAMANDER
to 5½ in. (140 mm)

SISKIYOU MOUNTAIN SALAMANDER
to 4¾ in. (120 mm)

117

NEW MEXICAN GROUP of woodland salamanders consists of a single species fitting structurally and geographically between the slender eastern and far western groups, but resembling more the far western.

JEMEZ MOUNTAINS SALAMANDER (*Plethodon neomexicanus*). Limited to forests of Jemez Mts., New Mexico, 8,500–9,000 ft. Lives in logs and under debris. Back and sides brown, belly gray. Costal grooves 18–19, usually 18; 6–8½ costal folds between appressed limbs. Fifth rear toe is mere stub, with 0–1 phalanx.

SLENDER EASTERN GROUP of woodland salamanders consists of five slim-bodied species. They are found in moist woods under leaves, bark, and logs. All but Weller's have 17 or more costal grooves, 5–10 between appressed limbs. Snout-to-vent length is equal to six or more head widths in contrast to less than six in robust eastern group (p. 120).

WELLER'S SALAMANDER (*Plethodon welleri*). Limited to a few southeastern mountain forests. Smallest of the slender easterns. Has 16 costal grooves, 3–4 costal folds between appressed limbs. Black back is adorned by blond or pearly patches.

NETTING'S SALAMANDER (*Plethodon nettingi*). Black back with a dusting of pale spots; dark belly. Lacks back stripe and mottled belly of some other slender eastern species. Costal grooves, 17–20; 5–7 costal folds between appressed limbs. Two subspecies: (1) *P. n. nettingi*— usually 18 costal grooves, profusely spotted back, limited to Cheat Mts., West Virginia; (2) *P. n. hubrichti* (now considered a full species, Thunder Ridge Salamander)— usually 19 costal grooves, densely spotted on back, limited to Peaks of Otter, Virginia.

RAVINE SALAMANDER (*Plethodon richmondi*). Dark above, with flecks of pearl or burnished gold; almost unmarked below. Occasionally has red back stripe. Costal grooves, 18–23, usually 20–23; 9–10 costal folds between appressed limbs. Three subspecies: (1) *P. r. richmondi*—usually 21 or more costal grooves; (2) *P. r. shenandoah* (now considered a full species, Shenandoah Salamander)—usually 20 costal grooves; (3) *P. r. hoffmani* (now considered a full species, Valley and Ridge Salamander)—whiter chin than *richmondi*.

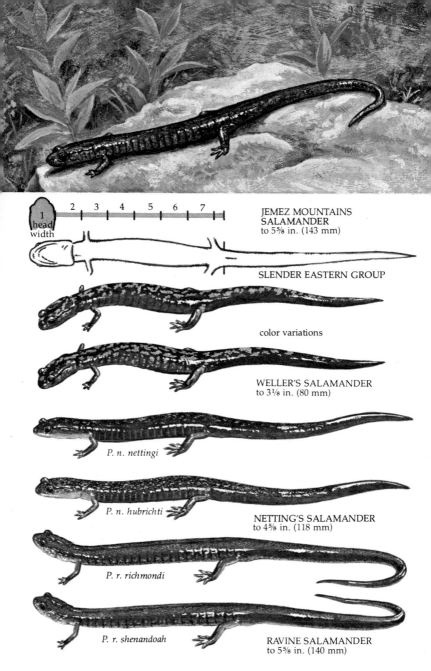

JEMEZ MOUNTAINS
SALAMANDER
to 5⅝ in. (143 mm)

1 head width

2 3 4 5 6 7

SLENDER EASTERN GROUP

color variations

WELLER'S SALAMANDER
to 3⅛ in. (80 mm)

P. n. nettingi

P. n. hubrichti

NETTING'S SALAMANDER
to 4⅝ in. (118 mm)

P. r. richmondi

P. r. shenandoah

RAVINE SALAMANDER
to 5⅝ in. (140 mm)

ZIGZAG SALAMANDER (*Plethodon dorsalis*). Name is from jagged or undulating yellowish to reddish stripe running down back, but "lead-backed" individuals are dark all over and lack the stripe. In all, the underside is strongly mottled with black and orange, which distinguishes Zigzag from Red-backed. Zigzags have 17–19 costal grooves, usually 18; 6–7 costal folds between tips of appressed limbs. Two subspecies: (1) *P. d. dorsalis*—back stripe wide, with zigzag or scalloped edges; (2) *P. d. angusticlavius*—back stripe narrow, with straight edges.

RED-BACKED SALAMANDER (*Plethodon cinereus*). Yellow to red stripe above, extending far onto tail; also, a so-called lead-backed variety entirely dark above and along sides. All red below or fine light-dark mixture. Costal grooves, 17–22; 7–10 costal folds between tips of appressed limbs. Two subspecies: (1) *P. c. cinereus*—stripe edges straight, usually 19 costal grooves; (2) *P. c. serratus* (now generally considered a full species, the Southern Red-backed Salamander)—stripe edges indented, usually 18 or 19 costal grooves.

ROBUST EASTERN GROUP of woodland salamanders includes seven species with stout bodies and broad heads. All have 17 or fewer costal grooves and up to three costal folds between appressed limbs; snout-to-vent length is less than six times head width.

WEHRLE'S SALAMANDER (*Plethodon wehrlei*). Frequents damp forest debris and rocks of high terrain; likes cave areas. Back dark brown or black; small paired red spots in some southern specimens. Sides dark, with pale streaks or dots; grayish below; white patch or patches on throat. Toes partly webbed. Has 16–17 costal grooves, 2–3 costal folds between tips of appressed limbs. (Related is *P. punctatus*, the White-spotted Salamander, with pale flecks above and 17–18 costal grooves; habitat NW Virginia and adjacent NE West Virginia.)

SLIMY SALAMANDER (*Plethodon glutinosus*). Found in woods under damp debris, also in shale crevices and rocky banks. Black above, with white to yellow spots, sometimes yellow or gray on sides; belly dark. Skin sticky. Has 16 costal grooves, 0–3 costal folds between tips of appressed limbs. Two subspecies: (1) *P. g. glutinosus*—dark throat; (2) *P. g. albagula*—light gray throat.

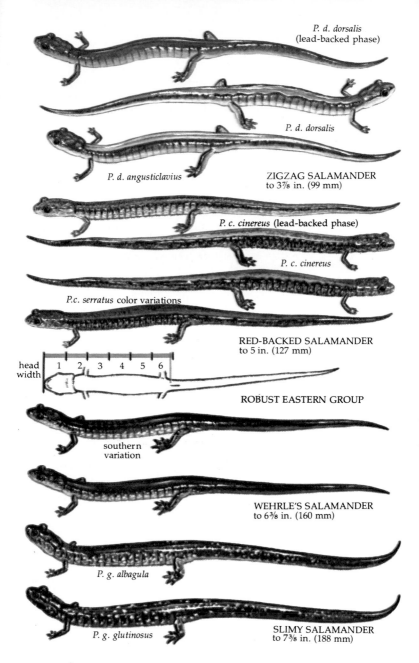

P. d. dorsalis
(lead-backed phase)

P. d. dorsalis

P. d. angusticlavius

ZIGZAG SALAMANDER
to 3⅞ in. (99 mm)

P. c. cinereus (lead-backed phase)

P. c. cinereus

P.c. serratus color variations

RED-BACKED SALAMANDER
to 5 in. (127 mm)

head
width

1 2 3 4 5 6

ROBUST EASTERN GROUP

southern
variation

WEHRLE'S SALAMANDER
to 6⅜ in. (160 mm)

P. g. albagula

P. g. glutinosus

SLIMY SALAMANDER
to 7⅜ in. (188 mm)

121

JORDAN'S SALAMANDER (*Plethodon jordani*). Lives under debris in thick forests, 900–6,400 feet. Color varies greatly. Back black, sometimes dotted with silver; young occasionally have paired red spots on back. Belly black or pale. Sides may have white or yellow marks. Cheeks, legs, throat, shoulders may be red or red-flecked. Has 15–16 costal grooves, 2–3 costal folds between tips of appressed limbs.

CREVICE SALAMANDER (*Plethodon longicrus*). Found in deep crevices in rock faces of granite gneiss, at 1,400–1,700 ft., in dense forest on NE slope of Bluerock Mt., a mile ESE of Bat Cave, North Carolina. Back black to red-brown, dappled or replaced with tan to light brown; belly dark, throat a little lighter; all surfaces may have white flecks. Costal grooves, 16; appressed limbs overlap 1–3 costal folds. Now thought to be same species as Yonahlossee.

YONAHLOSSEE SALAMANDER (*Plethodon yonahlossee*). Found under debris on wooded mountain slopes at 3,200–5,000 ft. Adults mostly reddish to brownish above; sides white or gray, belly dusky with few to many small white dots, black head and tail. Young are pale below, have paired reddish dots on back. Costal grooves, 15–16; 0–1 costal folds between tips of appressed limbs.

RICH MOUNTAIN SALAMANDER (*Plethodon ouachitae*). Lives under litter in moist forest on N slopes of Ouachita Mts. of Oklahoma and Arkansas, N of Saline River. Black back may be patterned with tan, brown, or red; may be speckled with bronze or white. Black sides and tail may be flecked with yellow. Pale throat merges with dark below. Costal grooves, 15–17, usually 16; 1–3 costal folds between appressed limbs.

CADDO MOUNTAIN SALAMANDER (*Plethodon caddoensis*). Found under debris in moist forest of Caddo Mts., Arkansas, S of Saline River. Mainly black but speckled with white and sometimes mustard on back and especially on sides; throat and belly pale. Usually has 16 costal grooves and 0–1 costal fold between tips of appressed limbs.

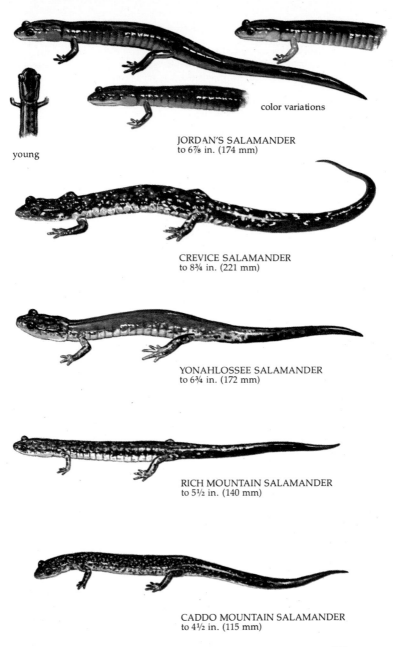

color variations

JORDAN'S SALAMANDER
to 6⅞ in. (174 mm)

young

CREVICE SALAMANDER
to 8¾ in. (221 mm)

YONAHLOSSEE SALAMANDER
to 6¾ in. (172 mm)

RICH MOUNTAIN SALAMANDER
to 5½ in. (140 mm)

CADDO MOUNTAIN SALAMANDER
to 4½ in. (115 mm)

CLIMBING SALAMANDERS—genus *Aneides*

All the *Aneides* are noted for jaw muscles so large that they make the head appear triangular-shaped when viewed from above. Upper teeth overhang the snout; tongue is fixed at forward end, free at rear.

The feet of these creatures are not webbed, and the innermost toe is much smaller than the other toes. Only the Green, Clouded, and Arboreal salamanders actually are climbers; their toes have conspicuously expanded tips. Eggs are laid on land, hatch into fully transformed individuals. There is no aquatic larval stage.

KEY TO CLIMBING SALAMANDERS

1. Found in E United States ....**Green,** below
   Found in W United States ....*see* **2**
2. Found in New Mexico ....**Sacramento Mountain,** below
   Found on Pacific slopes ....*see* **3**
3. Black or slate belly; 3–5 costal grooves between appressed limbs ....**Black,** below

(*not shown*) Lighter belly; 2 or fewer costal grooves between appressed limbs ....*see* **4**
4. Dusky, white-speckled belly ....**Clouded,** p. 126
   Whitish belly, unmarked ....**Arboreal,** p. 126

GREEN SALAMANDER (*Aneides aeneus*). Only climbing salamander in the East. Only salamander in the U.S. and Canada extensively green in color. Lives in moist clefts and fissures in rocks or climbs into cracks of trees. Back is black but overwhelmed by irregular pattern of sizable greenish patches. Belly commonly a light yellow, varies to bluish gray with scattered paler-hued flecks.

SACRAMENTO MOUNTAIN SALAMANDER (*Aneides hardyi*). Lives at 8,000–12,000 ft. in evergreen forest and tundra regions. Only N.A. salamander occurring in tundra. Toes round at tips and merely slightly larger than normal. Brown to blackish brown above, usually showing tan, beige or greenish blotches; beige to plum below.

BLACK SALAMANDER (*Aneides flavipunctatus*). Found under rocks and other objects near streams or seepages in mixed forests. Toes normal size, somewhat blunt but rounded tips. Characteristic color is black above, with or without pale marks. Gray to black belly and shorter limbs distinguish Black from Clouded and Arboreal salamanders (p. 126). Two subspecies now recognized (4 more may be confirmed eventually): (1) *A. f. flavipunctatus*—palely dotted or blotched above; (2) *A. f. niger*—black above, with or without speckled white.

124

IDENTIFYING CLIMBING SALAMANDERS

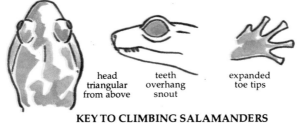

head
triangular
from above

teeth
overhang
snout

expanded
toe tips

KEY TO CLIMBING SALAMANDERS

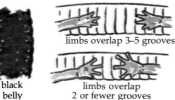

3

limbs overlap 3–5 grooves

limbs overlap
2 or fewer grooves

black
belly

4

dusky,
white speckled

whitish,
unmarked

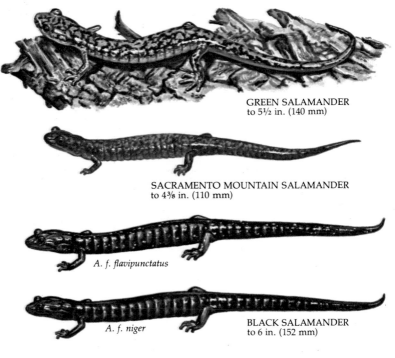

GREEN SALAMANDER
to 5½ in. (140 mm)

SACRAMENTO MOUNTAIN SALAMANDER
to 4⅜ in. (110 mm)

A. f. flavipunctatus

A. f. niger

BLACK SALAMANDER
to 6 in. (152 mm)

125

CLOUDED SALAMANDER (*Aneides ferreus*). Occurs in low-elevation forests under loose bark, in rock crevices, and in tree hollows. Has blunt toe tips, quite large; 16–17 costal grooves. May be uniform dark brown above, or brown may be all but obliterated by "clouds" of silver, metallic yellow or bronze, and dull pale green. Belly gray or brownish, speckled with white.

ARBOREAL SALAMANDER (*Aneides lugubris*). Lives in rotten logs, under debris, and under bark of trees up to 30 ft. high in low-elevation forests. Squeaks when disturbed, bites in defense. Tips of toes large and blunt. Brown above, sometimes spotted with yellow; whitish below. Costal grooves, 14–16, usually 15, distinguishing Arboreal from Clouded. Appressed limbs meet or almost meet.

OTHER LUNGLESS SALAMANDERS

RED HILLS SALAMANDER (*Phaeognathus hubrichti*). Lives in burrows in heavily wooded narrow belt across Alabama at S edge of Red Hills region. Long body, with 20–22 costal grooves, is distinctive. Adults are a uniform seal brown above and below. Eggs and young unknown; probably no aquatic larval stage. Rare and endangered.

SHOVEL-NOSED SALAMANDER (*Leurognathus marmoratus*). An interesting but seldom-seen inhabitant of clear upland brooks. Has an aquatic larval stage. Color above a uniform brown or gray to black, with two rows of large lighter-colored spots. Spots of one row usually alternate with spots of other row in staggered pattern. Belly light-colored in middle, dark toward sides. Head appears flattened. Top of tail carries sharp keel. Lower jaw is virtually immobile; head swivels upward to open mouth.

MANY-LINED SALAMANDER (*Stereochilus marginatus*). Found in pine barrens, usually under debris in pools, ponds, and swamps, occasionally on land nearby. Identification helped by alternating light and dark lines along sides, obscure in large adults; also by conspicuous sensory pits on top of head. Young bear a network of black or yellow above; dull yellow below, with profuse dark flecks. Adults are darker above. This species has 18 costal grooves, 8–9 between appressed limbs.

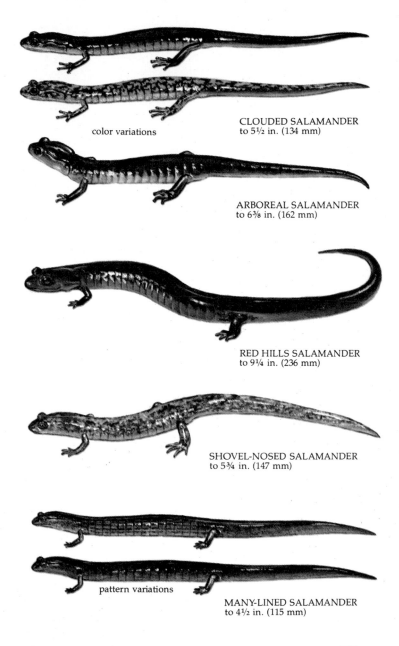

color variations

CLOUDED SALAMANDER
to 5½ in. (134 mm)

ARBOREAL SALAMANDER
to 6⅜ in. (162 mm)

RED HILLS SALAMANDER
to 9¼ in. (236 mm)

SHOVEL-NOSED SALAMANDER
to 5¾ in. (147 mm)

pattern variations

MANY-LINED SALAMANDER
to 4½ in. (115 mm)

DWARF SALAMANDER (*Manculus quadridigitatus*). Found under debris, usually near springs or in swamps. This small slim salamander resembles the brook salamanders (p. 98) but has 4 rather than 5 toes on each hind foot. Also, Dwarf larva's dorsal fin extends onto trunk of body rather than being restricted to tail as in larvae of brook salamanders. Costal grooves, 14–17; 5 grooves between appressed limbs. Occurs in 2 basic colorations: (1) pale, with broad mustard or darker band down back, brown sides, yellow belly; (2) dark, with pale streaks or lines on dark brown sides, scattered dark flecks and light areas on belly.

FOUR-TOED SALAMANDER (*Hemidactylium scutatum*). Inhabits woody or mossy margins of swamplands. Tail base visibly constricted, allowing tail to break off if grabbed so that salamander escapes. Four toes on hind feet; whitish belly has scatter of black dots. Commonly reddish brown to gray above and on sides; tail fin of larva extends forward onto trunk.

ENSATINA SALAMANDER (*Ensatina eschscholtzi*). Occurs mostly among stones, debris, and animal burrows of forests above 4,000 ft. Differs from other salamanders in having both a constriction at base of tail and good development of all digits. When disturbed, the Ensatina arches back and tail, strikes a rigid pose. When threatened, it may squeak, may secrete a white sticky astringent fluid largely from the tail. Eggs are laid in moist places on land; young hatch fully transformed. Ensatinas exhibit a striking range of colors but belly is usually whitish or flesh-colored; bases of limbs are lighter than ends. Has 12–13 costal grooves. Seven subspecies are recognized: (1) *E. e. eschscholtzi*—back brown, sides orange to red, belly pale, eyes black; (2) *E. e. croceater*—bold yellowish patches on dark back; (3) *E. e. klauberi*—prominent broken bands of alternate black and yellow to orange; (4) *E. e. oregonensis*—back medium to dark chocolate, sprinkling of black on faded yellow belly; (5) *E. e. picta*—showy patchwork of yellow-orange and black or dark brown back and tail; (6) *E. e. platensis*—like *croceater*, but patches orange to red instead of yellow; (7) *E. e. xanthoptica*—brown back sometimes suffused with orange, belly orange, eyes partly orange.

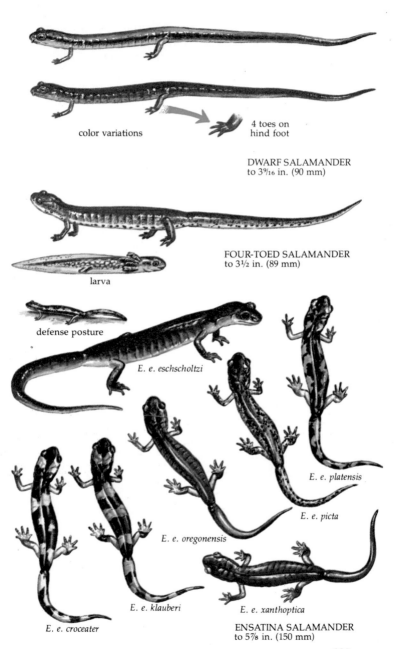

color variations

4 toes on
hind foot

DWARF SALAMANDER
to 3⁹/₁₆ in. (90 mm)

larva

FOUR-TOED SALAMANDER
to 3½ in. (89 mm)

defense posture

E. e. eschscholtzi

E. e. platensis

E. e. picta

E. e. oregonensis

E. e. klauberi

E. e. xanthoptica

E. e. croceater

ENSATINA SALAMANDER
to 5⅞ in. (150 mm)

NEWTS—family Salamandridae

Unlike other salamanders, newts have no costal grooves. Another unique characteristic is the arrangement of the palatal teeth in the roof of the mouth. Two long rows of palatal teeth extend from the level of the internal nares (nostrils), where the rows are close together, to a point back of the eyes, where the rows strongly diverge. The skin of adult newts secretes a poison that helps to protect them against predators.

Newts spend early life in the water as larvae but most pass at least part of their adult existence on land. The land-dwellers always return to the water to breed. Male newts returning to the water during the breeding season develop a smoother skin and a broader tail fin. These adaptations enable them to swim better. Breeding males also develop enlarged hind legs, dark pads on the toes, and a swelling around the vent. The enlarged legs and the toe pads make it easier for the males to clasp the females during the courtship embrace. The swollen vent is caused by a gland that enlarges to produce spermatophores filled with sperm to fertilize the female's eggs.

The newt family comprises two widely separated groups in North America: the western newts (genus *Taricha*) and the eastern newts (genus *Notophthalmus*). Western newts are restricted to the Pacific Coast region, eastern newts to areas east of the 100th meridian. The two genera also distinctly differ in coloration. Western newts are uniformly colored above; eastern newts are variously spotted, dotted, or striped above.

KEY TO NEWTS

1. (*not shown*) Uniformly dark back; found in Pacific Coast area ....*see* **2**
Spotted or striped back, found E of 100th meridian ....*see* **4**

2. Iris of eye entirely dark; belly tomato red; usually dark band across vent; undersurface of limbs about half dark ....**Red-bellied,** p. 134
Iris with conspicuous light areas; belly yellow or orange; usually no dark band across vent; undersurface of limbs much less than half dark ....*see* **3**

3. Upper and lower eyelids entirely dark; eyes small, usually not apparent in profile as seen from above ...**Rough-skinned,** p. 134

Lower eyelid at least partly light; eyes large enough to enter profile as seen from above ....**California,** p. 134

4. (*not shown*) Some dark spots on body and tail approaching size of eye ....**Black-spotted,** p. 132
Dark spots much smaller, dotlike, or none ....*see* **2**

5. Continuous red stripe — not prominently black-bordered — along each side of back ....**Striped,** p. 132
Broken stripe with conspicuous black border ....*N. v. dorsalis,* p. 132
Large black-bordered red spots ... .*N. v. viridescens,* p. 132
Red spots, no black borders ....*N. v. louisianensis,* p. 132

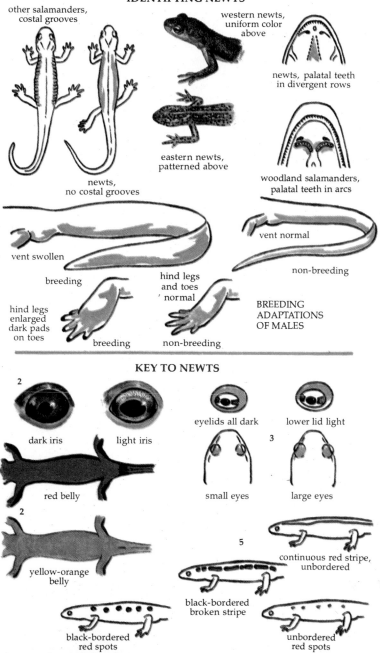

IDENTIFYING NEWTS

other salamanders, costal grooves

western newts, uniform color above

newts, palatal teeth in divergent rows

eastern newts, patterned above

newts, no costal grooves

woodland salamanders, palatal teeth in arcs

vent swollen

vent normal

breeding

non-breeding

hind legs and toes normal

hind legs enlarged dark pads on toes

breeding

non-breeding

BREEDING ADAPTATIONS OF MALES

KEY TO NEWTS

2

dark iris

light iris

eyelids all dark

lower lid light

red belly

3

small eyes

large eyes

2

yellow-orange belly

5

continuous red stripe, unbordered

black-bordered broken stripe

black-bordered red spots

unbordered red spots

EASTERN NEWTS—genus *Notophthalmus*

Eastern newts include three species. In spring, the females lay eggs singly, attaching them to objects in ponds or quiet pools or streams or swamps, particularly those abounding in submerged vegetation. Larvae hatch from the eggs and by late summer usually lose their gills and transform into young newts, called efts. These leave the water and spend one to three years on land. Efts are red and have thick rough skins. They are often encountered in the woods, especially after rains. When mature, efts change from red to greenish brown, return to the water to breed, and remain there for the rest of their lives.

In some areas at some times, efts are neotenic—that is, they transform only partly and reach sexual maturity while in the water. Neotenic individuals retain gill stubs or gill slits or both throughout life.

EASTERN NEWT (*Notophthalmus viridescens*). Yellow below; yellow to olive or brown above, with many black dots over all surfaces. Red markings vary with subspecies. Eft is orange to red or cinnamon above, yellowish white to yellow-orange below, usually with red markings like adults. Neotenic Eastern Newts are common in Southeast, rare elsewhere. Found in or near swamps, small streams, forest pools. Four subspecies: (1) *N. v. viridescens*—row of black-edged red dots on each side of back; (2) *N. v. dorsalis*—red stripe, black-edged and discontinuous, on each side of back; (3) *N. v. louisianensis*—either no red marks or else red dots without complete black edges, yellow to olive above; (4) *N. v. piaropicola*—same as *louisianensis* except dark brown to black above; eft rare.

STRIPED NEWT (*Notophthalmus perstriatus*). Olive to brown back, sharply demarcated from yellow belly during adulthood. May or may not be marked with small sparse black dots. Eft is orange-red. In both adult and eft, a red stripe, either continuous or broken, runs along each side of the back. Neotenic form not uncommon.

BLACK-SPOTTED NEWT (*Notophthalmus meridionalis*). Devoid of red. Olive-hued above, with small to large dark spots; yellow-orange to orange below. Pale yellow line runs along each side of back; sides have scattered yellow spots. No red markings. Larvae transform directly into adults, skipping eft stage and remaining in water. U.S. subspecies: *N. m. meridionalis*.

TYPICAL LIFE HISTORY OF NEWTS

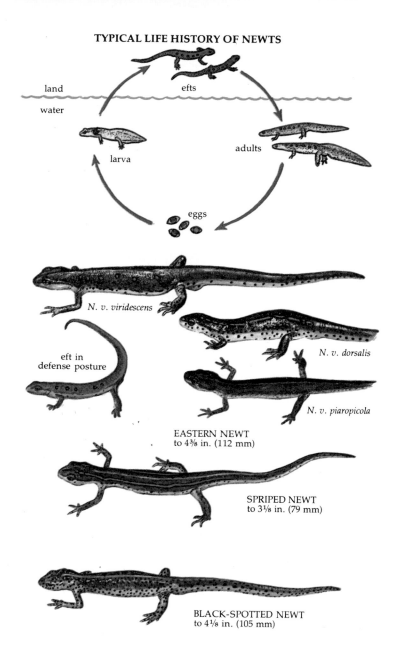

land

water

efts

larva

adults

eggs

N. v. viridescens

eft in
defense posture

N. v. dorsalis

N. v. piaropicola

EASTERN NEWT
to 4⅜ in. (112 mm)

SPRIPED NEWT
to 3⅛ in. (79 mm)

BLACK-SPOTTED NEWT
to 4⅛ in. (105 mm)

133

WESTERN NEWTS—genus *Taricha*

Western newts spend adult life mostly on land. In late winter or early spring they converge on pools and slow-flowing streams, mate, deposit their eggs, then return to land. In five to ten weeks the eggs hatch into pond-type larvae with long gills and a tail fin extending far forward onto the trunk. During the same summer in which they were hatched, or perhaps during the following summer, the larvae lose their gills and transform into young newts. These emerge from the water and become land-dwellers, reaching sexual maturity during the third year.

Adults generally have a warty skin. During the breeding season, however, males temporarily develop a smoother skin. When first captured, a western newt arches its back and raises its head and tail. This exposes its bright belly, which may serve as a warning to predators of the newt's poisonous skin secretion.

ROUGH-SKINNED NEWT (*Taricha granulosa*). Breeds December–July in still pools, sluggish brooks, slack backwaters. At other times frequents woody or rocky litter. Back mustard, black, or brown; belly yellow to red. Palatal teeth from inverted **V**. Eggs laid singly. Larvae have balancers. Two subspecies: (1) *T. g. granulosa*—few or no dark patches on belly; (2) *T. g. mazamae*—many dark patches on belly.

CALIFORNIA NEWT (*Taricha torosa*). Breeds December–May in streams and permanent standing waters; at other times is found nearby under debris. Tan to dark brown above, yellow to orange below. Palatal teeth form inverted **Y**. Eggs are laid in masses. Larvae have balancers. Southern populations are excessively warty, due to disease. Two subspecies: (1) *T. t. torosa*—dark areas in iris are much wider than pupil; (2) *T. t. sierrae*—dark areas in iris are about same width as pupil.

RED-BELLIED NEWT (*Taricha rivularis*). Usually seen only when breeding (February–May) in swift brooks and rivers of redwood areas to 7,000 ft.; other times occasionally seen around tree roots nearby. Back brown to black, belly vivid red. Deep-hued patch on vent and underside of legs. Eyes large, enter profile when viewed from above. Palatal teeth form inverted **Y**. Eggs laid in masses. Larvae have degenerate balancers or none.

IDENTIFYING WESTERN NEWTS

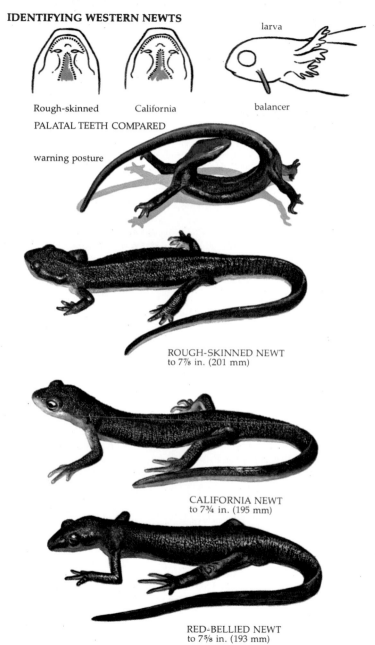

larva

balancer

Rough-skinned   California

PALATAL TEETH COMPARED

warning posture

ROUGH-SKINNED NEWT
to 7⅞ in. (201 mm)

CALIFORNIA NEWT
to 7¾ in. (195 mm)

RED-BELLIED NEWT
to 7⅝ in. (193 mm)

135

AMPHIBIAN EVOLUTION, DISTRIBUTION, AND ANATOMY

Amphibians are intermediate between fishes and reptiles, sharing features of both. Amphibians first appeared on earth some 350 million years ago, in the geological period known as the Devonian. Derivatives of fishes, they were the first land-dwelling vertebrates. Some 15 major groups developed over the next 125 million years, but none of these early groups survived beyond about 180 million years ago. The three modern orders, known from the fossil record of no earlier than 150 million years ago, have survived because of their confinement and adaptation to habitats largely spurned by reptiles, birds, and mammals.

Two of the three modern orders of amphibians occur in North America north of Mexico: the frogs and toads (order Salientia, or Anura) and the salamanders (order Caudata). Caecilians (order Gymnophiona) form the third group and are represented only in the tropics. Frogs, toads, and salamanders are well represented in the fossil record and appeared at about the same time.

The earliest adaptation enabling amphibians to live out of water was modification of the two pairs of lateral fins, used by fishes for swimming, into two pairs of limbs for locomotion on land. Vital to a complete and successful invasion of land were three other adaptations: ways of breathing air, the prevention of dehydration by loss of water through the skin, and mechanisms to permit development of eggs on land. Amphibians never solved very well the last two of these problems. They are thus confined to a life close to water, but can move on land and can breathe air. The name *amphibian* denotes the sort of double life they lead.

The successive life stages of most amphibians are: (1) egg, (2) larva, (3) subadult, and (4) adult. All except the egg are usually free-living. Metamorphosis from larval to subadult stages is rapid; between other stages, more gradual. A recently metamorphosed subadult is not sexually mature, requiring considerable growth and maturation before it can reproduce.

Distribution

Amphibians' habitats are more ephemeral and their enemies more numerous than those of other vertebrates. Amphibians survive in part because of their generally high level of fecundity—lower than in most fishes but much higher than in other terrestrial vertebrates. Fickle weather, perhaps their greatest enemy, tempts them in favorable times to spread widely, then mercilessly reduces their numbers in times of drought.

Because amphibians depend on high humidity for survival, they are most abundant as both species and individuals in areas with high rainfall. They are highly intolerant of salt water. They cannot survive where no refuges exist below the frost line.

Skin

Amphibians molt every day or at least every few days, shedding the dead outer layers of skin—usually in one piece. Often the layers are pulled off with the mouth, then swallowed. For this reason, the shed skin is seldom seen even in captive amphibians. The skin bears numerous glands, secreting mostly mucus and poison. A few tropical frogs have oil glands. Spread over the body by the hands and feet, the oil aids greatly in reducing evaporation of moisture from the skin.

Pigment cells (chromatophores) in the skin permit color change (metachrosis) in many species, particularly in frogs and toads and less so in salamanders. In the skin's outermost layer are yellowish or reddish fatty pigments (lipophores). Immediately beneath these are the guanophores containing crystals or platelets that give rise to whitish, green, and blue colors. The lower layer of melanophores contains black or brown pigment, called melanin. Melanophores have highly branched slender projections that surround the other chromatophores. In response to hormones, the melanin either disperses to varying degrees in the projections of the melanophores, producing a dark color, or aggregates and produces a light coloration. Lipophores are somewhat amoeboid and capable of burrowing among the guanophores or even covering them completely.

Skeleton, Limbs, and Locomotion

Anurans rarely have true teeth in the lower jaw, and some have none even in the upper jaw. Salamanders and caecilians are well provided with teeth in both jaws. In some salamanders, males have distinctly larger teeth than do females.

Salamanders have 30 to 100 vertebrae; anurans only 6 to 10; caecilians as many as 250. All have a single cervical (neck) vertebra. Salamanders and anurans have a single sacral (pelvic) vertebra. Salamanders have numerous tail vertebrae; in anurans, they are modified as a single elongate bone, the urostyle. Caecilians have one to three tail vertebrae, the anus virtually terminal. The ribs are short in caecilians and salamanders, absent in all except the most primitive of the anurans.

In anurans, the hind legs are, as a rule, much larger and stronger than the forelegs, which enables them to jump or leap. The tibia and fibula are fused, and the proximal metatarsals are elongate—in some families, fused as one rodlike bone. Despite these adaptations, some true toads and other anurans prefer to "walk" on all fours. The forelimbs and hind limbs of salamanders are more or less equal but rather weak. In sirens, hind limbs are absent, but the girdle persists internally. In amphiumas, the limbs are ludicrously tiny. Caecilians lack both limbs and girdles. Some salamanders use the tip of the tail as an aid in locomotion, curving it forward and then pushing with it.

Regeneration

Fishes and amphibians (but not reptiles, birds, or mammals) can regenerate body parts accidentally lost—often in as short a time as a few weeks. The mechanisms involved are still poorly understood. A knowledge of regeneration might help in restoration of lost parts or limbs in humans and might be an important clue to protracted life—the "fountain of youth."

Digestive System

An amphibian's digestive system is basically like that of other vertebrates. In anurans, the intestines shorten greatly in metamorphosis, changing from the very long form in herbivorous tadpoles to a short tube in carnivorous subadults and adults.

The tongue, usually attached at the front of the mouth, is poorly developed in aquatic amphibians, well developed in terrestrial adults. In some anurans and many salamanders, it is attached all around the floor of the mouth or only at the rear. Some salamanders have a mushroom-shaped tongue attached by a narrow stalk.

Respiratory System

In amphibians much respiration takes place through the skin, which must be kept moist because a useful exchange of gases cannot occur across a dry membrane. Anuran tadpoles have internal gills; salamander larvae, external gills. Adults and subadults all have simple lungs; in some salamanders (including the plethodontids), they are reduced or absent. Lacking a rib cage, amphibians use the floor of their mouth as a pump.

All amphibians have a larynx, but only in anurans does it produce sounds, a function best developed in males. Males call (some cannot) in the breeding season. One or two resonating sacs on the throat are inflated while calling. Calls are distinct and identifiable to species, so help prevent interspecific mating.

Circulatory System

In all amphibians the heart is basically five-chambered (not three as commonly stated), containing: a posterior sinus venosus, an anterior conus arteriosus, and three "core" chambers of two partially divided atria and an undivided ventricle. The relatively few red blood cells are large (amphiumas have the largest of any vertebrate), and have nuclei except in some salamanders and anurans.

Excretory and Reproductive Systems

Amphibians have kidneys essentially the same as those of most fishes. In anurans the urinary bladder is large, but it is lacking in salamanders and caecilians.

The gonads are relatively large but smaller than those of fishes. Both egg-laying (oviparous) and live-bearing (viviparous) species occur in all three living orders of amphibians.

Nervous and Sensory Systems

The brain is primitive, with a very small cerebellum that controls and is correlated with the simple locomotion of amphibians. As in fishes, there are 10 pairs of cranial nerves.

The sensory system is much like that of other vertebrates. A lateral line system similar to that of fishes is present in aquatic species and also in aquatic developmental stages. Sensitive to changes in pressure, this system informs the animal of the depth at which it is swimming and acts as a sort of radar mechanism for detecting objects.

Ears are well developed only in anurans. Salamanders and caecilians have evidence of ears but can detect only vibrations conducted through the limbs or water. Some anurans also lack a tympanum and apparently have little or no ability to hear airborne sounds.

Some salamanders are blind—notably cave-dwelling or artesian species. But all anurans and most salamanders have well-developed eyes. Terrestrial species have eyelids, generally absent in aquatic species in which a transparent skin covers the eyes. The lower eyelid is more mobile than the upper (if present), and there is no true third eyelid, or nictitating membrane. The pupil may be round, oval, or slitlike, and either vertical or horizontal. The iris is varicolored and often specific as to species. To focus the eyes, amphibians (like fishes) shift the position of the lens in relation to the cornea rather than by changing the shape of the lens.

Taste buds are scattered over the tongue and the interior of the mouth. Smell is activated by a pair of vomeronasal organs opening into the mouth, as well as by a pair of nasal organs opening to the exterior at the tip of the snout. The tongue transfers particles in solution on its surface to the vomeronasal organs.

REPRODUCTION

Male frogs and toads commonly aggregate in spring or summer at suitable bodies of water and establish choruses. Often several species will be at the same body of water. A pattern of call dominance is usually established, much like the peck order among birds or the dominance sequence in social animals.

Soon after the chorusing is started, females appear and seek out the males of their species, identifying them by their calls. The male clasps the female with his forelegs either at the level of her armpits (axillary amplexus) or just in front of the hind legs (inguinal amplexus). He fertilizes the eggs as they are laid by the female, which may be in a few hours, or days later. Many species lay their eggs underwater, others on land or in vegetation. The eggs are then abandoned, and the female goes her way. Species adapted to life in arid or semi-arid regions usually breed in temporary pools and have an extremely brief period of development. Males of these species have exceptionally loud voices.

Both species and sex recognition are primarily by voice among the anurans, but are visual and olfactory in salamanders. In mixed groups, a breakdown of audio cues results in some crossbreeding; however, species capable of hybridization seldom breed in the same congresses, using either different sites or breeding at different times.

In a few species, sperm is transferred directly from the male to the female prior to egg laying. Only one—the Tailed Toad—has a copulatory organ that inserts sperm into the female's cloaca. Other anurans with internal fertilization (all foreign species) have only cloacal contact.

Male salamanders have either no voice or only a rudimentary one. They find mates either by migration to ponds or other communal breeding sites in spring, or by coincidental encounter in their normal activities. Most male salamanders produce spermatophores, and they perform a complex behavioral ritual to entice a female to retrieve them. A male plethodontid salamander rubs his sexually stimulating chin gland against the female's body or holds it against her, usually in the pelvic area. The male newt rubs against the body of the female repeatedly as he swims by her. Then he clasps the female between his enlarged hind limbs which, in the mating season, have rough black corneous surfaces that enable him to grip her securely. He drags the female about for several minutes or for as long as an hour. Once convinced that she is sufficiently stimulated to follow, the male walks ahead of her, lifting his tail and dropping one or more spermatophores as he walks. As the female follows, she momentarily rests her cloacal opening over each spermatophore. The sperm are attracted chemically to receptacles in the walls of the cloaca, and, when the eggs are deposited, fertilization takes place. Most salamanders achieve fertilization in this manner.

In a few species—notably the amphiumas—the spermatophore is transferred directly from male to female by cloacal contact, much as in birds. Only in the most primitive groups—sirens, giant salamanders, and members of the family Hynobiidae (Asiatic)—does the male simply extrude sperm over the eggs as they are laid.

Eggs

In anurans, the number of eggs laid per season varies from one to as many as 30,000 (in true toads, *Bufo*). In salamanders, the greatest number laid is a few hundred. In all amphibians the number is higher in species laying eggs in water, where the survival hazards are greater, than in those laying eggs on land. The eggs of amphibians that breed on land must be laid close to water to which the larvae can quickly find their way to finish their transformation to subadult. Alternatively, the eggs must be provided with sufficient nutrients so that the larval stage and transformation can be passed in the egg.

Among North American anurans, only the narrow-toed toads lay eggs on land, but many species of salamanders do so. Some salamanders lay their eggs singly in water. A few salamanders and most toads lay them in a pair of strings, one from each oviduct. Most frogs lay their eggs in clumps, others as a surface film.

Growth and Longevity

The larval life of an amphibian may be as short as 10 days, as in spadefoot toads, which are adapted to development in temporary, fast-drying pools in dry regions, to as long as three years, as in the Bullfrog in northern states. Some salamanders remain in a larval stage throughout life, except for their reproductive systems, which mature in two to four years. Most amphibians reach breeding age in one to two years. They continue to grow throughout life, but their growth after sexual maturity is greatly slowed.

Most small amphibians have a life span of three to six years, medium-sized species of eight years, and species of Amphiuma and Siren of up to 15 years. Anurans appear to live longer than do salamanders of comparable size.

BEHAVIOR

The behavior of amphibians is not complex, but it is nevertheless surprisingly varied. Social behavior is, in general, rudimentary in amphibians. Tadpoles and salamander larvae sometimes form aggregations, possibly getting some benefit from a slight rise in temperature as a result of the grouping. Parental care, which is not as common in temperate regions as in the tropics, involves either the male or the female lingering near the eggs until they hatch. In anurans, there is little evidence of benefit derived from this attention. Most salamanders remain with their eggs, and some—the Hellbender, for example—guard them aggressively. The male Hellbender eats some of the eggs in exchange for giving them protection. Female plethodontid salamanders, *Necturus*, and the Marbled Salamander brood their eggs, but the young remain with the female (or vice veɩsa) in only a few cases.

Dispersal

All organisms tend to disperse, thus escaping competition and the overcrowding that leads to severe discomfort and high death rates. The higher the death rate, however, the more rapid the successful genetic combinations. All organisms have also evolved mechanisms that minimize the excessive production of offspring, but the control system usually allows for enough of an excess so that some selection pressure is maintained at all times. Each generation probes its boundaries and tests its relative competence, maintaining a high level of survival efficiency and occupying suitable habitats. In favorable years, a species may extend its range considerably beyond the limits of unfavorable years.

Amphibians often breed in aggregations that are far too dense to permit survival of the individuals for more than a few weeks, and often they pass winters in high densities. As a result, a pattern of migration (often only a few hundred yards) is developed—from winter quarters to breeding grounds, then to a feeding area and finally back to winter quarters.

Territoriality and Homing

After the brief breeding season, individual amphibians direct all their energies toward personal survival. They seek shelter for hiding during the day and emerge at night to find food. They are rarely active in daytime.

Territoriality in amphibians is studied relatively little, but virtually all species appear to maintain at some time during the year a territory that is defended to some degree from intruders of their own species.

Their home range includes the territory plus adjacent areas into which they wander from time to time. Home ranges may be only a few square inches to perhaps 100 square feet in most salamanders, from 100 to 400 square feet in anurans. Species that breed within their normal home range defend their territories most tenaciously.

Many amphibians have a strong homing instinct. How they navigate or orient themselves in homing is not fully understood, but some are known to use celestial cues—the sun or the moon, but apparently not the stars alone. Otherwise, they move randomly.

Temperature Control

Like fishes and reptiles, amphibians are ectotherms—that is, they have little means of controlling their body temperature. Excessive cold immobilizes them, and they succumb to somewhat lower high temperatures than other vertebrates. Most amphibians are capable of at least slow movements at temperatures that are completely numbing to most reptiles. Their prime vehicle for thermoregulation is behavior: heat is gained by basking in the sun (insulation), by conduction from the surface supporting them, and by convection from the air. They lose heat by radiation, conduction, convection, and evaporation.

States of Dormancy

Amphibians survive winter in temperate regions by seeking refuge. No amphibian can tolerate freezing temperatures for more than a few hours. In a refuge where the humidity is high and the temperature remains above freezing—even if by only a fraction of a degree—amphibians go into a state of physiological dormancy called brumation, as distinguished from the true hibernation of birds and mammals (endotherms). Brumation sites include the bottoms of bodies of water sufficiently deep never to freeze, and holes or crevices leading to ground levels below the frost line where there is sufficient moisture. All respiration takes place through the skin.

A similar dormancy called estivation occurs in places where excessive heat is maintained for long periods. Estivation sites may be much the same as those for brumation but with coolness and high humidity the prime requisites.

ENEMIES AND SELF-DEFENSE

Amphibians are notoriously lacking in protective devices. Except for the quick-jumping frogs, they cannot escape even by speed. They have no claws, no powerful tail, no notable capacity to bite hard, no active means of poisoning or otherwise harming potential predators. Their sole protections are a somewhat slippery body, a usually small and inconspicuous form, secretive habits including nocturnal activity, sometimes a piercing scream, and a passively poisonous skin. They are the prey of virtually everything bigger than they are. On land, they are persecuted ceaselessly by birds, reptiles, and mammals; in water, they are the prey of fishes. Their very survival is miraculous, but it is a seemingly perpetual miracle.

No amphibians can introduce their poisons into the body of another animal, but the skin poisons of some amphibians are potent enough to kill or to sicken most animals. They may even be fatal to other kinds of amphibians if the animals are confined together. Shorebirds have been observed ganging up on one toad, taking turns swallowing it—none able to keep it down—until the poison is eventually wiped off well enough so that one bird can hold it down without regurgitation. Hognosed snakes and their relatives evolved a resistance to toad poisons by an enlargement of the cortisone-secreting component of the adrenal gland. They also have special structures for feeding on toads, their principal diet. Most snakes would die at once if they were to eat a toad. Even those snakes that eat toad or frog eggs, which are not poisonous, reject the adults.

Marine Toad skin poison is fatal to humans, dogs, and most other animals that bite or eat them. The highly complex poison consists of some powerful adrenalinlike fractions that are absorbed quickly by the mucous membranes of the mouth and throat. They may speed the heart rate so much that an uncontrolled and lethal flutter results. If an animal survives this shock and the poisons are swallowed, the adrenalinlike substance is destroyed immediately in the stomach. Equally powerful digitalislike fractions that are not harmed by digestive juices are then absorbed through the walls of the digestive tract. They slow the heartbeat so much that it may stop. These and other amphibian skin poisons are just as lethal in the bloodstream as in the digestive tract. Primitive tribes use them to poison arrows, spears, and stakes. In humans, some frog poisons produce severe bouts of sneezing and copious nasal secretions if they are inhaled or come in contact with the nasal membranes. After handling amphibians, it is very important to wash your hands and to make certain you do not touch your eyes or other membranes while any of the skin secretions are on your hands.

Bright warning colors are often associated with powerful skin poisons (notable exceptions are the true toads). Many anurans have "flash"colors that are normally covered but that are exposed when the animals leap. The colors disappear when the animals fold their legs in midair, thus deceiving possible predators.

In a minor way, amphibians can be a threat to themselves. Large anurans are likely to gobble up anything that moves, even eating their own young and other small anurans or salamanders. Large salamanders are equally voracious, but mostly within narrower limits. One whole genus of salamanders, *Gyrinophilus*, feeds primarily on other salamanders. Some larvae of the Tiger Salamander and its relatives, as well as some of the tadpoles of at least one species of the western spadefoot toads, may eat others of their kind. As a result of this high-protein diet, these cannibals become very large—20 to 30 times normal size—and have highly muscularized jaws and toothlike serrations on the edges of the jaws. They also either defer or lose completely their ability to transform.

Ecological Status

All adult amphibians eat insects and other small invertebrates, are much at home around water where pest control is most desired, and have larvae that either have the same diet or that eat algae and other soft plant material underwater. They are truly valuable members of the ecosystem, but, with few exceptions, are disregarded or scorned.

The success of amphibians could be assured for millions of years to come, with probably a steady increase in their diversity, except for depredations by man. The most insidious of man's activities is habitat alteration and destruction, such as the conversion of lands into agricultural use, the building of towns, roads, and scattered installations, and the pollution of rivers, lakes, and swamps or their draining, filling, diverting, or drowning behind dams. In the Great Plains, however, even the most intensive agricultural practices do not eradicate all species of amphibians. Rains produce temporary pools in which the amphibians can breed. At other times of the year, these species burrow to depths out of reach of plows and cultivators.

It is indeed fortunate that amphibians are so secretive. Because they pose no special threat, they are not deliberately persecuted, except for those species sought intensively for food, study, and demonstration.

The prognosis for amphibians is that many of the species with limited distributions will become extinct. Those living in rugged habitats resistant to human alteration will probably persist, and a few inconspicuous species will remain widely distributed. Total eradication of amphibians is not likely, but their diversity will be greatly diminished. There appears to be no practical means of preventing this outcome.

Economic Value

All over the world, frog legs are considered a delicacy. As a result, the larger species are near extinction and, in some areas, they are protected by law. In North America, for example, the Bullfrog is now protected in most states. The Bullfrog was limited originally to eastern North America but has in recent years been introduced widely into northern Mexico, all of western United States, Hawaii, Japan, Australia—wherever it might establish itself and become a food resource. Any amphibian is edible—even those with poisonous skin secretions, if the skin is removed without touching or transferring any of the secretions to the flesh of the amphibian.

In some areas, amphibians are believed to have therapeutic values, ranging from aphrodisiacs to curatives and palliatives. Most such beliefs are erroneous, but the amphibians are exploited nevertheless. The scientific use of amphibians has so far been negligible, but because of the complexity, diversity, and potency of their toxins, the potential for the future is great. Chemicals that are pharmacologically similar to digitalis, epinephrine, and norepinephrine exist in the skin secretions of amphibians and have properties of stability that make them superior to the well-known drugs they resemble.

Amphibians are not always welcomed and valued additions where they are introduced. Both the Bullfrog and the Marine Toad, for example, have preyed not only on insects but also on small vertebrates, including valued native amphibians, drastically reducing their numbers. Marine Toads introduced into new habitats to combat agricultural pests have caused the deaths of pets, domestic animals, and even a few humans because the unfamiliar toads have been eaten like native frogs—no care having been taken in the removal of the deadly toxic skin. Introduction of the Clawed Frog (*Xenopus*) in western United States, primarily from discards following the abandonment of their use for pregnancy tests, has been so highly successful that some native species are threatened.

KEEPING LIVE AMPHIBIANS

Captive amphibians should be provided with the same general living conditions that they have in nature—either high humidity or water, plus adequate food and clean quarters. Glass aquariums usually make the best cages, even for land-dwellers, because the humid environment can be duplicated with a minimum of evaporation. A glass plate suffices for a cover. Many amphibians can crawl up vertical surfaces and escape if their quarters are not securely covered. To let in air and to keep the humidity from becoming too high, put several layers of short strips of tape on each side at the top edges of the aquarium to lift the glass plate a fraction of an inch.

Avoid using tap water, which contains chlorine and other antibiotic additives that are highly toxic. Rain water is best. If tap water must be used, it can generally be made safe by letting it stand in an open container to "age" for several days. Most tap water can also be made safe immediately by adding dechlorinating drops, available at commercial aquarium dealers.

Infections are a hazard in keeping amphibians in captivity. The most common is "red leg," a bacterial infection that irritates the skin and turns it red. The skin may also produce copious secretions. Red leg is fatal unless controlled promptly. A very weak salt solution helps prevent and cure the disease. A solution too strong is toxic to amphibians, however; if it is too weak, it is ineffective. The best and recommended treatment is a 0.025 solution of tetracycline administered orally in very small quantities—5 mg in 0.2 ml of distilled water for each 20 grams of body weight. For a Leopard Frog, this is 0.2 cc; for a Bullfrog, 1 cc. This is given twice daily for five to seven days. During this time the amphibians are not fed and are kept relatively warm (22–$27°C$; 72–$80°F$). Tetracycline added to the water or injected into the amphibian does no good and may actually be harmful. While undergoing treatment, the frogs should be kept in a sloping-bottomed container half covered with water, which is changed daily.

Except for tropical species, a temperature of 20–$25°C$ (68–$77°F$) is preferred. Higher temperatures may be harmful. Amphibians are much more resistant to low temperatures (never below freezing, however) than to high temperatures, but it is well not to keep them below 10–$15°C$ (50–$59°F$).

Avoid crowding. Too many individuals will foul the quarters rapidly, making it necessary to dismantle and clean the container frequently. If a careful and elaborate simulation of the natural habitat has been provided, cleaning can be laborious. The alternative, however, is losing the animals. Plants can be grown in leakproof containers sunk into the soil. Climbing frogs and salamanders need large plants or branches on which they can exercise. All amphibians need places to hide at times.

A jar or a plastic box makes a very simple temporary container. Put a small amount of water in the bottom and add a rock, a piece of wood, or some other object onto which the animals can crawl to rest. These containers can be cleaned frequently.

Aeration of the water for aquatic types, tadpoles, or other larvae is helpful, but not as important as it is for most fishes. Likewise, the water temperature is not as critical as it is for fishes, but it should be somewhere between 15 and 25°C (59–77°F). Even an occasional variation beyond these levels is not likely to be fatal unless the temperature drops below 5°C (41°F) or exceeds 30°C (86°F).

All adult terrestrial amphibians are normally carnivorous and must be fed live foods. Just about anything that moves and can be swallowed is acceptable. Remove uneaten prey as quickly as possible to prevent pollution of the quarters.

Aquatic amphibians are guided as much by odor as by movement in finding food, and so they will accept bits of meat, worms, or fishes as well as whole live prey. Tadpoles are largely herbivorous, eating mostly algae and tender plants. Wilted romaine or escarole lettuce are good foods. Spinach is not good (produces kidney stones), though it is often recommended. Supplement this vegetable diet with small cubes of raw or boiled liver two or three times a week. Keeping an aquarium clean obviously requires considerable care.

It is very difficult to keep any amphibian through its complete life cycle—even to nurture tadpoles through transformation to maturity. Anyone attempting to do so should study carefully the publication by George Nace on the breeding, care, and management of laboratory animals (see p. 151).

Remember to wash your hands after handling amphibians, and to make certain you do not touch your eyes or other membranes while any of the skin secretions are on your hands.

Because of the serious depredations of the natural populations of most kinds of plants and animals, including amphibians, some stringent regulations that limit the collection and possession of both domestic and foreign species have been enacted by the federal and state agencies responsible for fish and game animals and other natural resources. Before you collect amphibians in any area, you should consult these agencies to learn what regulations apply.

STUDYING AMPHIBIANS

Amphibians can be studied in nature as they go about their normal activities, in captivity by observing actions that more or less approximate their behavior in nature, and by experimentation both in nature and in the laboratory.

1. *Nature.* Far more useful observations can be made of amphibians in nature than of those in captivity. Few data, for example, are available on the seasonal activities of frogs and the climatic factors that influence them. A record of the beginning dates of chorusing and when it stops, of dates with greater or less volume, and of the major atmospheric variations associated with these and adjacent dates is easily compiled and becomes uniquely useful. Dates of egg laying, egg hatching, transformation—all are worthy of record. Rate of growth, age of sexual maturation, average and maximum longevity, average duration of breeding behavior, courtship behavior, rates of dispersal, sites and dates of brumation and emergence, daily and seasonal activity patterns, demographic cycles—these are other kinds of data to be collected from observations in nature.

Little is known about orientation for homing, how territories are maintained, how individuals or species interact in both the breeding and non-breeding seasons, how the places to brumate are selected, to what degree communal grouping occurs during brumation or at other times, how members of the same species and of the same or opposite sex are recognized, what enemies exist and how they are avoided, what diseases and parasites plague natural populations, why there are periodic abundances—these and other observations are needed to give us more knowledge about amphibians and how they live.

An intensive study of any natural population sometimes requires marking individuals for recognition. The best technique is injection of tattoo ink under the skin of the tail or some other part of the body with a fine hypodermic needle and a syringe. The ink is injected as the needle is withdrawn, and the length and color of the streaks can be varied to conform to a code that permits numbering hundreds or thousands of individuals without duplication. The animals should be under anesthesia when the injections are made. Depending on the size of the individual, it is immersed for 1–10 minutes in a 1:3000 solution of tricaine methanesulfonate (MS 222). Recovery occurs in 5–20 minutes.

2. *Captivity.* Much the same questions can be asked about amphibians kept in captivity as about those studied in nature. But the answers obtained in one situation may not be valid in the other. Observations in captivity, however, are often the best source for a hypothesis leading to the same or similar observations in nature.

3. *Experimentation.* Not all experimental studies, either in nature or in captive animals, require the sacrifice of the subject. Experimental studies in nature that do not involve injuring the animals may include, for example, moving the animals to different localities to test orientation and homing ability. Provision of artificial sanctuaries, food supplies, or stimuli are other possibilities. Captive specimens may contribute to many controlled-factor experiments in which the animals are not harmed and can be released in their natural habitat when the experiments are concluded. (See "Ethics for the Enthusiast," p. 9.)

Some professional laboratory studies do require sacrifice of the subject, however. In such cases, the most humane method of killing the animals is with a non-irritating anesthetic. Tricaine methanesulfonate (MS 222) is the best. Exposure to ether, injection with pentobarbital, immersion in weak alcohol (25–35 percent ethyl alcohol), or brain and spinal-cord pithing are much less desirable alternatives, neither quick nor free from irritation. Chloroform, hyperthermia, and hypothermia should never be used.

When, in spite of the best of care, a captive specimen dies unexpectedly, or when a dead or dying specimen is found in the field, the techniques that may be used to preserve it are extremely simple. As soon as possible after death, put the animal on a paper towel in a shallow tray, then arrange its body and appendages in the desired position. Pour over it a 10 percent formalin solution, immersing the body shallowly. Cover it with another paper towel that has been soaked in the same solution. In a few hours the animal will harden and become "fixed." It can then be transferred to a sealed container in which the hardening is permitted to continue for a few days. After this conditioning, put the specimen in a 65 percent solution of ethyl alcohol (or 30 percent methyl alcohol) for permanent storage. Or it can be left in the formalin, which unfortunately tends to discolor specimens in time. The addition of a pinch of baking soda to each cup of 10 percent formalin helps to preserve the natural color for a longer time.

For a museum or any other permanent reference collection, the specimen should be labeled with a tag tied with strong thread just below the knee joint. The tag is made of a waterproof paper on which is printed, in waterproof ink, either a number referring to a catalog where all pertinent data are recorded, or the data themselves. Most important are the date and the locality of capture. Without this information, a specimen is useful only as an example of its species or as material for anatomical study.

OTHER SOURCES OF INFORMATION

A nearby museum or college is one of the best sources for more information about amphibians. In addition, there are a number of organizations that will answer inquiries:

Division of Herpetology
Museum of Natural History
University of Kansas
Lawrence, Kan. 66045

Division of Herpetology
Field Museum of Natural History
Roosevelt and Lake Shore Drive
Chicago, Ill. 60605

Division of Herpetology
Museum of Vertebrate Zoology
University of California
Berkeley, Cal. 94720

Division of Herpetology
American Museum of Natural History
Central Park West at 79th Street
New York, N.Y. 10024

Division of Herpetology
National Museum of Natural History
Washington, D.C. 20560

There are three national professional organizations: the American Society of Ichthyologists and Herpetologists, the Herpetologists League, and the Society for the Study of Amphibians and Reptiles. Each publishes one or more journals. If you are interested, inquire about these organizations at one of the addresses above.

The following publications also offer more information:

Altig, Ronald. "A key to the tadpoles of the continental United States and Canada." *Herpetologica,* Vol. 26 (2): pp. 180–270. 1970.

Conant, Roger. *A Field Guide to Reptiles and Amphibians of Eastern and Central North America.* Boston: Houghton Mifflin, 1975.

Czajka, Adrian F., and Max A. Nickerson. *State Regulations for Collecting Reptiles and Amphibians.* Milwaukee Public Museum, Special Publications in Biology and Geology, 1. 1974.

Dowling, Herndon G. *1974 Yearbook of Herpetology.* New York: American Museum of Natural History, 1975.

Goin, Coleman J., and Olive B. Goin. *Introduction to Herpetology.* 3rd. ed. San Francisco: W. H. Freeman, 1978.

Lofts, Brian. *Physiology of the Amphibia.* Vols. II and III. New York: Academic Press, 1974, 1976.

Moore, John A. *Physiology of the Amphibia.* New York: Academic Press, 1964.

Nace, George W., et al. *Amphibians: Guidelines for the Breeding, Care and Management of Laboratory Animals.* Washington, D.C.: National Academy of Sciences (2101 Constitution Avenue, N. W.), 1974.

Neill, Wilfred T. *Reptiles and Amphibians in the Service of Man.* Indianapolis: Bobbs-Merrill, 1974.

Noble, G. Kingsley. *The Biology of the Amphibia.* New York: McGraw-Hill, 1931. (Reprinted by Dover, 1954.)

Oliver, James A. *The Natural History of North American Amphibians and Reptiles.* New York: Van Nostrand, 1955.

Porter, Kenneth R. *Herpetology.* Philadelphia: W.B. Saunders, 1972.

Stebbins, Robert C. *Amphibians of Western North America.* Berkeley: University of California Press, 1951.
_____. *A Field Guide to Western Reptiles and Amphibians.* Boston: Houghton Mifflin, 1966.

Vial, James L. *Evolutionary Biology of the Anurans.* Columbia: University of Missouri Press, 1973.

INDEX

Individual species names, both common and scientific, are indicated with the text page only, since the text, illustrations, and range maps pertaining to each species run side by side. Although this is primarily a species index, orders and families are also included.

To find common names, look under the general headings "Frogs," "Toads," or "Salamanders," as appropriate. Common names are also listed under family and group headings. For instance, Brimley's Chorus Frog will be found under the headings "Treefrogs" and "Chorus Frogs" as well as the general heading "Frogs."

To find scientific names, look for the genus first and then the species or subspecies.

For an explanation of the names used in this book, see page 14.

154

155

A B C **D** E F